THE LAST COMMUNION OF SAINT JEROME

THE LAST COMMUNION OF SAINT JEROME

The Eucharist, Monasticism, *and* Priesthood *in the* Life *of a* Church Father

DOM BASIL NIXEN, OSB

TAN Books
Gastonia, North Carolina

Unless otherwise noted, Scripture quotations are from the Douay-Rheims versoin of the Bible. Available in the public domain.

Cover design by Jordan Avery

Cover image: *The Last Communion of Saint Jerome by Rafael Tegeo Díaz* (ca. 1829), oil on canvas. Album / Alamy, used with permission.

ISBN: 978-1-5051-3670-8
ePUB ISBN: 978-1-5051-4010-1

Published in the United States by
TAN Books
PO Box 269
Gastonia, NC 28053

www.TANBooks.com

Printed in the United States of America

Quod nos dicimus: Dominus regit me, Hebræi dicunt: Dominus pascit me, et nihil mihi deerit. Qui Deum habet, et qui Deo adhæret, nihil boni deest ei.

—Ex Breviario in Psalmos, Psalm XXIII

Contents

Introduction: Pretiosa in conspectu Domini

Although we have abundant information about St. Jerome's life, we possess no account of his death from the immediate eyewitnesses who were present on the occasion. As he lay dying on that final day of September,[1] we can reasonably surmise that he was attended to by certain monks of his monastery, in particular, his brother Paulinian and Eusebius of Cremona. It is also likely that St. Eustochium, his devoted spiritual daughter, was also present and took care of him as her very father in his last moments. It is likely that he gave one last spiritual exhortation to these spiritual children, and that it approximated in tone and content the words of St. Paul to Timothy (2 Tim. 4:1-8) preserved for us in the Mass for a Doctor:

> Dearly beloved: I charge thee, before God and Jesus Christ, who shall judge the living and the dead, by his coming, and his kingdom: Preach the word: be instant in season, out of season: reprove, entreat, rebuke in all patience and doctrine. For there shall be a time, when they will not endure sound doctrine; but, according to their own desires, they will heap to themselves teachers, having itching ears: And will indeed turn away their hearing from the truth, but will be turned unto fables. But be thou vigilant, labour in all things, do the work of an evangelist, fulfil thy ministry. Be sober. For I am even

> now ready to be sacrificed: and the time of my dissolution is at hand. I have fought a good fight, I have finished my course, I have kept the faith. As to the rest, there is laid up for me a crown of justice, which the Lord the just judge will render to me in that day: and not only to me, but to them also that love his coming.

It is also likely that he received viaticum, perhaps from his brother Paulinian, who was a priest, and that he did so with great fervor and devotion, and afterwards died in peace, with the sentiments of St. Simeon in his heart—*Nunc dimittis, Domine* (Now lettest thou thy servant depart in peace, O Lord).

Based on these few elements that could have reasonably accompanied the passing of St. Jerome, some pious soul of the fourteenth century composed an elaborately florid account of this event and attributed his legend to St. Jerome's historical disciple, Eusebius of Cremona (see Migne's *Patrologia Latina* (PL) 22: col. 239-282). This pious author, whoever he was, knew enough about St. Jerome to give some impression of authenticity, but the evident mistakes he makes in establishing the chronology of Jerome's life and other inaccuracies of the account make it clear that his report is not history, properly speaking, but an imaginative and pious conjecture as to what St. Jerome's passing *must have been like*. The memorable culmination of the pious account is the moment when St. Jerome receives his last Communion surrounded by angels, and breathes forth his last after praying the *Nunc Dimittis*.

Regardless of its validity as "history" properly speaking, this legend of St. Jerome's death, *De Morte Hieronymi*, became a popular devotional text that helped many people grow closer to God and increased their devotion to St. Jerome. In 1491, a translation of the legend appeared in Florence, *Il Devoto Transito del Glorioso Sancto Hieronymo, Ridocto in Lingua Fiorentina, a contemplatione delle devote persone,* and became a treasured souce of meditation for many people, including the famous painter Sandro Botticelli. Shortly after its publication, Botticelli painted a small (25 cm wide and 35 cm tall) painting of St. Jerome's last Communion for Francesco Del Pugliese, a Florentine merchant. The painting was originally known as *Il Transito di San Girolamo,* a clear indication that it was inspired by the famous legend concerning St. Jerome's death. Through the centuries the painting passed from owner to owner until arriving at its current resting place in the Metropolitan Museum of Art in New York City.[2]

Botticelli's small devotional painting eventually sparked a train of more elaborate descendants. In 1611, the Bolognese painter Domenico Zampieri, commonly known as Domenichino, executed a majestic altar piece with St. Jerome's last Communion as its theme for the Church of San Girolamo della Carità in Rome, closely imitating, yet far excelling, the earlier work by his teacher, Agostino Carracci. Domenichino's famous painting, much larger than Botticelli's and incorporating more of the sensational elements from the legend of St. Jerome's death, is now housed in the Vatican Museums, and an immense mosaic representation of the work adorns the altar of St. Jerome in Saint Peter's Basilica. The piece has an arresting effect, and often makes a vivid impression on those walking through Saint Peter's Basilica. The worshipping love of St. Jerome for the Holy Eucharist is unquestionably conveyed by the magnificent work.

Nevertheless, due to their connection with the fourteenth century legend *De Morte Hieronymi,* these artistic masterpieces representing the last Communion of St. Jerome are often the target of trivializing comments by modern scholars, and one often gets the impression that the subject of St. Jerome's last Communion had no historical basis whatsoever. But such a simplification of the issue ignores the truth that there is always a connection between historical truth and "that halo of legend that inevitably forms round the heads of all the striking personalities of history."[3] In the following work, I would like to establish that link, and show why a devotion to the *last Communion* of St. Jerome is thoroughly consistent with who the historical man actually was. I would like, therefore, to meditate on St. Jerome's teaching on and love for the Holy Eucharist, and on the unconventional manner in which he lived his priesthood, in the hopes that the literary and artistic theme of St. Jerome's last Communion will be better appreciated and understood as a way that the Catholic tradition grappled with, proclaimed, and reverently safeguarded a truth about one of its most beloved saints that was not so easy to understand.

Chapter 1

The Eucharist as Exegetical Key to Understanding Scripture

St. Jerome left us no systematic treatise on the Eucharist. His teaching on the subject is scattered throughout his immense literary output. For our immediate purpose, we may divide the relevant passages into two categories: first, those that emphasize the Eucharist as an exegetical key to understanding Scripture; and second, those that delineate the means by which we can attain a proper disposition to receive the Eucharist. A good place to begin is his commentary on Ecclesiastes. In the midst of his explanation of Ecclesiastes 3:13, "For every man that eateth and drinketh, and seeth good of his labour, this is the gift of God," he makes the following statement:

> Since the flesh of the Lord is true food, and his blood is true drink, according to the anagogical sense, this alone is our good in the present age, if we are nourished by his flesh and drink his blood, not only in the mystery (Eucharist), but also in the reading of the Scriptures. Indeed, true food and drink gathered from the Word of God is the knowledge of the Scriptures.[4]

Here St. Jerome distinguishes between a *sacramental* eating of the Eucharist and a *spiritual* communion with Christ's Body and Blood through assiduous reading of the Bible. Although both means lead to spiritual union with the Word of God, he makes clear in his commentary on the Gospel of St. Matthew (Matt. 26:26) that the Eucharist objectively makes present the truth of His Body and Blood, and is thus a superior mode of Christ's presence:[5]

> After the figurative Passover had been fulfilled, and He had eaten the flesh of the lamb with His apostles, He takes bread, that strengthens the heart of man (cf. Ps. 103:15), and passes over to the sacrament of the true Passover, so that as Melchisedech, priest of God Most High, had done offering bread and wine as a type in anticipation of Him (cf. Gen. 14:18), He likewise should make the offering in the truth of His body and blood.[6]

The sacramental presence of Christ's Body and Blood in the Eucharist was not limited to the Last Supper, however; indeed, the faithful have the privilege of receiving it daily should they so choose. St. Jerome thus explains the fatted calf that is slaughtered to provide for the banquet upon the return of the prodigal son (Luke 15): "The fatted calf which is slaughtered for the penitent's salvation is the Savior Himself, on whose flesh we daily feed, whose blood we drink."[7]

In the allusion to the fatted calf we see how the Eucharist was an exegetical key often employed by St. Jerome to explain obscure passages in Scripture. The Scriptures themselves, therefore, point the reader beyond themselves, to seek Christ's Body and Blood in the Sacrament. This is more frequently to be observed in St. Jerome's exposition of the Old Testament, which was particularly dear to him. Commenting on the description of the new temple in Ezechiel 41:7, he sees in the upper room (*cœnaculum*) described in the temple a foreshadowing of the upper room where Christ instituted the Eucharist:

> The Savior of mankind also celebrated a Passover in a higher chamber, it too was a large and wide upper room, purged of all uncleanness and strewn, prepared for a spiritual banquet, where He bequeathed the mystery of His body and blood to His disciples, and left us the eternal festivity of the immaculate lamb.[8]

The Eucharist is a key to understanding the Scriptures because it is the glorified Body and Blood, and, hence, Soul and Divinity, of Jesus Christ, who alone opens the Scriptures for us. In a majestic passage in which he displays his consummate ability to explain the Scriptures, St. Jerome shows how closely the Eucharist is linked to the person and mission of Christ. The passage in question is again taken from the Prophet Ezechiel:

> And he brought me back to the way of the gate of the outwards sanctuary, which looked towards the east: and it was shut. And the Lord said to me: this gate shall be shut, it shall not be opened, and no man shall pass through it: because the Lord the God of Israel hath entered in by it, and it shall be shut. For the prince. The prince himself shall sit in it, to eat bread before the Lord: he shall enter in by the way of the porch of the gate, and shall go out by the same way (Ez. 44:1-3).

St. Jerome explains the passage as follows:

> This door, therefore, which is closed to everyone (for no man shall pass through it), shall be closed to the prince, and to the duke, and shall be opened by the coming of Him who shall sit in it, that He might eat bread before the Lord. Concerning this bread He speaks openly in the Gospel, saying: My food is to do the will of Him who sent me, that I may accomplish His work (John 4:34). He is the prince, and pontiff according to the order of Melchisedech, and victim and priest, who with us eats celestial bread in the Father's sight, and drinks the wine of which He speaks in the Gospel: I shall not drink of the fruit of this vine, if not when I drink it anew in My Father's kingdom (Matt. 26:29): in that kingdom, namely, concerning which He says elsewhere: The kingdom of God is within you (Luke 17:21).
>
> And the door shall be closed. Nobody, indeed, can know the sacraments of the Lord's passion, of His body and blood, on account of the majesty of the reality. And our Prince is of such goodness and clemency, that though He sits alone at the door, which is closed, He desires to have numerous companions at His table and banquet, and says: Behold, I stand at the door and knock; if someone should open to me, I shall enter near him and dine with him, and he with me (Apoc. 3:20). Alone He eats bread before the Lord, for His substance and divine nature is distinct from all substances of creatures. He enters and exits through the same door of the atrium: for He is both within and without, that is, infused inside and surrounding everyone; and entering through the

> door, that with Himself He may lead in others, who without His teaching and assistance cannot enter; and exiting, that He may lead in others yet again; and speak to them who do not grasp the harder matters. But that the Eastern door beyond the limits of the world should be forever closed, and never be exposed to human sight, John's Gospel verifies when saying: No one has ever seen God: the only-begotten Son who is in the bosom of the Father, He has made Him known (John 1:18).[9]

The passage which gave rise to the Eucharistic interpretation in the previous passage was taken from Ezechiel 44:3: "The prince himself shall sit in it [i.e., the doorway], to eat bread before the Lord." Although the text here mentions only bread, i.e. the Eucharistic Body of the Lord, St. Jerome instinctively brings into his interpretation the sacred Blood, which is concomitant with the Eucharistic Body. We see Jerome similarly introduce the Lord's Eucharistic flesh when commenting on Ezechiel 45:19, a passage which alludes only to the precious Blood:

> And, the prophet says, the priest shall take of its blood, which shall be for the sin of everyone: who in Exodus and in the Gospel by similar words is called a lamb, with John the Baptist proclaiming: Behold the Lamb of God who takes away the sins of the world (John 1:29). The blood, however, is that same precious blood by which we are redeemed in the passion of the Lord Savior; by whose flesh we are nourished, and whose blood we drink.[10]

The concomitance of the Lord's Flesh and Blood, and, moreover, water, help Jerome explain why Isaiah invites the thirsty poor of Israel to *eat* the water, wine, and milk which they are to procure gratuitously in the prophecy: "All you that thirst, come to the waters: and you that have no money, make haste, buy and eat. Come ye: buy wine and milk without money and without any price" (Is. 55:1). The *doctor maximus* (St. Jerome) explains this passage thus:

> What is more, in a wonderful manner they buy waters without money; and they do not drink them, but eat them. Indeed, He who came down from heaven, is both water and bread (Jn. 6). Thus, that which is read in some codices: *Buy, and drink,* was changed by uninformed scribes, who considered it more coherent that water should be drunk rather than eaten. There is, moreover, evil money, or silver, which the Scripture condemns when it says: *Money which is given with deceit shall be reputed as a potsherd (Prov. 26:23 according to the Septuagint);* and in another place: *Your silver is condemned (Jer. 6:30).* There is also silver which is compared to the words of God: *The sayings of the Lord are pure sayings: silver tried by the fire, purified seven-fold (Ps. 11:7).* Having thus rejected that silver and money with which we cannot purchase the waters of the Lord, let us press onwards to Him, who, holding the chalice of the Sacrament, spoke thus to His disciples: *Receive and drink, this is my blood, which shall be shed unto the remission of sins (Matt. 26:27-28).* This is the wine which Wisdom mixed in her bowl, inciting all the foolish ones, who lack the wisdom of this age and world, to drink. And we should purchase not wine alone, but also milk, which signifies the innocence of little ones, which custom and figure is kept to

> the present day in Western Churches, so that wine and milk are offered to those reborn in Christ. Concerning this milk Paul also used to say: *I gave you milk to drink, not solid food (1 Cor. 3:2).* And Peter: *In the manner of new born babes, long for spiritual milk (1 Pt. 2:2).* Hence Moses, also, understanding wine and milk as referring to Christ's passion, testifies with mystical words: *His eyes are more lovely than wine, and His teeth are whiter than milk (Gen. 49:12).* In place of "milk" here the Septuagint translated "fatness". Concerning this fatness saint David says in the Psalm: *Let my soul be filled with fatness and grease (Ps. 62:6)*; and in another place: *He fed them with fatness of wheat, and satisfied them with honey from the rock (Ps. 80:17).* This fatness seems to be nothing other than the sacramental flesh to which the Lord summoned His disciples, saying: *Unless you eat my flesh, and drink my blood, you will not have life within you (John 6:54).*[11]

This passage shows how the Eucharist is perhaps the greatest expression of God's extravagant love for us. As the enduring memorial of His passion and death on the Cross, it not only makes present for us the Christ who suffered, but fills those who worthily partake of the Eucharistic banquet with the water and blood which flowed from the pierced side of Christ. He asks us for nothing else in return than that we bear His "easy yoke" and "light burden," i.e., that we avoid that which separates us from Him, and seek out that which unites us to Him. But we consistently perceive His restful load to be unbearable, and therefore miss out on the festive joy the Eucharist is meant to bring us. St. Jerome thus interprets the words the Lord echoes through the prophet Hosea, "And I will be to them as one that taketh off the yoke that is on their jaws: and I bowed down to him that he might be nourished" (Hos. 11:4), as foreshadowing the sorrow of Christ's unrequited love in giving us the Eucharist:

> And they considered my light yoke to be terribly heavy: and I bowed down to them, deserting the heavenly realms, that I might eat with them, having assumed the form of man, and gave to them the food of my Body, which is both food and shared rejoicing *(cibus et conviva)*.[12]

However, those who receive the Eucharist as the magnificent gift it truly is are thereby strengthened to ascend to that heavenly realm from which the Son of God descended in order to give it to us. Anyone who attempts the arduous climb to heaven without this fortifying food will therefore collapse from weakness on the way. This is the mystical truth St. Jerome perceives behind the miracle of the multiplication of the loaves in Matthew 15:32:

> Jesus does not wish to send them away hungry, lest they faint on the way. Whoever, therefore, hastens to reach the desired dwellling place without the heavenly bread is in peril. Hence the angel also says to Elijah: *Rise, and eat, for you are setting out on a great journey (3 Kings 19:7).*[13]

This passage shows us how important viaticum (one's last Communion before death) was for Jerome, as it has been for Catholics throughout the centuries. We can only imagine, then, that he would have taken great care to make sure he received it before his own death, and that he did so as devoutly and worthily as possible. Indeed, he was keenly aware of the truth St. Thomas Aquinas would declare centuries later in his sequence for the Feast of Corpus Christi:

> Good souls consume it, as do evil: unequal, though, their destiny: life or destruction. Death for the evil, life for the good: behold, though equal the reception be, vastly unequal is the outcome.[14]

St. Jerome expressed this truth in his polemical treatise against Jovinianum:

> The sanctification in the sacraments is one for master and servant, nobleman and commoner, king and soldier: though that which is one may be differentiated according to the merits of the recipient. *He, indeed, who unworthily eats and drinks, will be answerable for the desecrated Body and Blood of Christ (1 Cor. 11:27).* Or do you suppose that since Judas, too, drinks from the same chalice as the other Apostles, he will deserve the same merit with the rest?[15]

St. Jerome returns to St. Paul's admonition from 1 Corinthians in his dialogue against the Pelagians. Toward the end of Book I, amidst numerous texts from the Pentateuch affirming man's inherent tendency toward sin after the fall, Jerome makes a connection between someone who, through ignorance, eats from ritual sacrifices of which he is forbidden to do so by the laws of Leviticus 22:10-13, and St. Paul's example of someone consciously in a state of sin partaking of the Eucharist:

> Finally it says: *If someone eateth of the sanctified things through ignorance, injustice and transgression is imputed*

> *to him, and he shall be answerable for the burnt-offering.*[16] Hence the Apostle also admonishes that the Eucharist of the Lord is to be eaten with caution, lest we eat it unto our condemnation and judgment (1 Cor. 11:27). If ignorance is condemned in the law, how much more full knowledge in the Gospel![17]

The worthy reception of the Holy Eucharist was, therefore, very important for St. Jerome. We shall now turn our attention to passages in which he discusses how we may fittingly dispose ourselves to receive it.

Chapter 2

What it Means to Receive the Eucharist Worthily

To begin with, it must be noted that St. Jerome did not regard the human person as ever being "worthy" of receiving the Lord in Holy Communion. It is always a sheer grace, a manifestation of God's mercy in condescending to be united with His creature. He illustrates this point quite forcefully in the dialogue against the Pelagians when explaining the Lord's prayer, which by Apostolic tradition has always been prayed by the priest before Communion:

> The Apostles pray for the forthcoming *bread* that is *daily* or *above all substances,* that they might be worthy of the reception of the body of Christ. Whereas you, through abundant holiness and confident uprightness, audaciously arrogate to yourselves the heavenly gifts. Thereupon follows: *Forgive us our debts, as we also forgive our debtors.* Those rising up from the baptismal font, and born anew into the Lord Savior, fulfilling that which is written concerning them: *Blessed are they whose injustices are remitted, and whose sins are covered (Ps. 31:1),* immediately, when making their first communion with the body of Christ say: *And forgive us our debts,* debts which were already forgiven in the confession of Christ;

> whereas you are arrogant and proud owing to the purity of your holy hands, and glory in the refinement of your speech. However perfect be the conversion of a man, and complete his possession of virtues after vices and sins, can such people be as free of vice as those who immediately proceed from the font of Christ? And yet they are commanded to say: *Forgive us our debts, as we also forgive our debtors (Matt. 6:13):* not in false humility, as you construe, but in the trembling of someone dreading his awareness of human fragility.[18]

If, therefore, even those who are newly baptized, and as free from sin as is humanly possible, cannot receive the Eucharist worthily, what does it mean to receive the Eucharist worthily for St. Jerome? Essentially, it means belonging to Christ and prefering nothing to Him and His love.

Worthy Reception Means Belonging to Christ

Let us first explore how a worthy reception of the Eucharist entails *belonging to Christ*. In order to do so, we must return to the first passage we looked at from the dialogue against the Pelagians, and do a bit of detective work to discover where in the Scriptures Jerome took the verse he juxtaposes with St. Paul's admonition from 1 Cor. 11:27. As far as I can tell, St. Jerome is quoting Leviticus 22:14. A comparison of the verse as quoted by the saint and the Scriptural texts at our disposal reveal a considerable difference. The Douay reads: "He that eateath of the sanctified things through ignorance, shall add the fifth part with that which he ate, and shall give it to the priest into the sanctuary," which is a direct translation of the Vulgate: "*Qui comederit de sanctificatis per ignorantiam, addet quintam partem cum eo quod comedit, et dabit sacerdoti in sanctuarium.*" The Greek of the Septuagint differs little,[19] and the RSV, which translates the Hebrew, renders also the meaning of the Septuagint: "And if a man eats of a holy thing unwittingly, he shall add the fifth of its value to it, and give the holy thing to the priest." The question thus presents itself: from where is Jerome taking the second part of the verse as he quotes it: *imputatur ei iniquitas atque delictum, et voti reus erit;* "injustice and transgression is imputed to him, and he shall be answerable for the burnt-offering?" Perhaps he is quoting from memory, and, though usually his memory is remarkably accurate, here he seems to confuse the second part of Lev. 22:14 with a phrase drawn from another part of Scripture that deals with the same topic; or perhaps he is quoting a manuscript tradition that is no longer extant. But it seems likely he is quoting the passage according to the *sense*, i.e., that although ignorance might mitigate moral culpability, it does not eliminate it altogether. The verse as quoted by Jerome emphasizes the moral responsibility for the trespass of having unlawfully, albeit ignorantly, eaten of the sacrifice. The verse as found in the Vulgate, Septuagint, and Hebrew, all underline the need to make *restitution* for the trespass committed, i.e., by repaying the priest not only the portion consumed, but also the fifth part of it in addition.

It is this final possibility that I would like to explore. By analyzing the verses from Leviticus 22 preceding the verse quoted by Jerome, we can understand the logic of the law governing the consumption of the sacrifices. To begin with, the law is operating on the principle that the burnt offerings are not only ritual expiatory sacrifices for the whole people, but also provide the sustenance for the priest and his family. As Lev. 22:7 explains, at sundown, having observed the precepts of purification, "the priest shall eat of the sanctified things, because it is his meat" (i.e., sustenance). Consequently, only those who *belong* to the offering priest can partake of the sacrifices. Lev. 22:10-13 thus specifies that no stranger or person foreign to the priest's household may partake of it: no sojourner or hired servant or even any married daughters of the priest, who, by virtue of their marriage, no longer belong to their father, but to their husband.[20] If, however, the daughters are widows or divorced, and no longer have a husband to whom they belong, they may return to their father's house and eat of the sacrifices, as they did previous to being married. In order to eat the sacrifices lawfully, therefore, one must legitimately belong to the priest as either spouse, child, or slave.

It is in this context that Jerome juxtaposes Lev. 22:14 with 1 Cor. 11:27: *Itaque quicumque manducaverit panem hunc, vel biberit calicem Domini indigne, reus erit corporis et sanguinis Domini*; "Therefore, whosoever shall eat this bread, or drink the chalice of the Lord unworthily, shall be guilty of the body and of the blood of the Lord." When read in the context of Leviticus 22, the verse from St. Paul is essentially saying that only those who belong to the offering priest, that is, to Christ, can lawfully partake of the Eucharist, and whosoever partakes of it not belonging to Him is *reus*, that is, guilty or answerable, for the sacrilege of having stolen something sacred—in this case, the Body and Blood of Jesus Christ. It seems, therefore, that in quoting Lev. 22:14, Jerome was actually reading back into it the language of St. Paul! It was thus not so much a lapse of memory as a manifestation of the tight Scriptural logic that governed his exegesis. Although he did not give the *ipsissima verba* (literal translation) of Leviticus 22:14, he did give the *ipsissima vox* (the very voice or meaning), for he was reading Leviticus in the light of St. Paul and vice-versa, and thus revealing the deeper meaning of both. By so doing, he helps us understand that only someone who belongs to Christ can "eat of this bread and drink the chalice of the Lord" worthily.

Worthy Reception Means Preferring Nothing to the Love of Christ

Objectively speaking, all the faithful belong to Christ and are constituted His members through faith in baptism. But given our ability to separate ourselves from Christ through sin, it is necessary to renew our belonging to Christ continually by choosing Him over other goods, and denying ourselves lesser goods so as to cling more perfectly to the highest good. Our Lord Himself says in the Gospel: "He that loveth father or mother more than me is not worthy of me: and he that loveth son or daughter more than me is not worthy of me" (Matt. 10:37). The Gospel of St. Luke, which usually emphasizes Christ's leniency and mercy, surprisingly formulates this evangelical principle in much harsher terms: "If any man come to me, and hate not his father and mother and wife and children and brethren and sisters, yea and his own life also, he cannot be my disciple" (Luke 14:26). This Gospel saying seems to have been at the heart of St. Jerome's life and vocation.[21] It helps explain the crises of conscience that often plagued him, and which dramatically exploded in the famous dream, or rather, nightmare, in which his conscience indicted him for preferring the writings of Cicero to Christ Himself.[22]

Apart from the Gospel, Jerome probably came across the principle as formulated by St. Anthony of the Desert, of whom St. Athanasius, his biographer, relates: "The Lord gave to Anthony the charism of speech; and thus, he comforted many who were sorrowful, led others who were in conflict into friendship, and exhorted all to prefer nothing in the world to the love for Christ."[23] And he certainly would have been familiar with the principle as formulated by St. Cyprian of Carthage, whose patristic authority Jerome highly esteemed. In his commentary on the Lord's Prayer, St. Cyprian admonishes us "to prefer nothing whatsoever to Christ, for neither did He prefer anything to us"; and, moreover, "to cling inseparably to His love."[24] Although centuries later St. Benedict of Nursia would make this principle a lapidary norm of his monastic *Rule—nihil amori Christi præponere* (RB 4)—neither he nor the previous tradition ever intended it to be limited to monks; rather, it was an axiom of Christian life that was valid for all—laity, hierarchy, and religious. And it was one that, from very early on, had particular bearing on the reception of the most Holy Eucharist.

By Jerome's time, fasting from all food and drink, including water, was a widespread means for the faithful to prepare themselves to receive the Eucharist. St. Augustine provides a clear witness to this phenomenon in a letter to Januarius:

> It is evident that when the disciples first received the body and blood of the Lord, they did not do so fasting. However, is the universal Church to be censured for the fact that now it is always received fasting? Indeed, it so pleased the Holy Ghost that in honor of such a Sacrament, the body of the Lord should enter the Christian's

> mouth before any other food: surely on that account this custom is observed throughout the entire world.[25]

In a letter to the learned Spaniard, Lucinius, Jerome discusses whether one should fast on Saturdays and whether the Eucharist should be taken daily. Although in his discussion the two subjects seem to be unrelated, closer inspection reveals that it is precisely the *Eucharistic* fast which is as the heart of the matter.

> As to your questions, the very eloquent man Hippolytus and other writers have written regarding the things that you inquired of me: whether or not one should fast on Saturday, and whether the Eucharist should be received daily, as is the custom in the Churches of Rome and Spain. But I think I should counsel you by saying that Ecclesiastical traditions (especially those that do not hinder faith) are to be observed in the manner in which they have been handed down from our forebears, and that the custom of some is not to be overthrown by the contrary custom of others. Moreover, it would be great if we could fast at all times, as we read in the Acts of the Apostles that the Apostle Paul and those who were with him did in Paschaltide and on Sunday (Acts 13;20;21). Yet they are not to be accused of the Manichean heresy, since carnal food should not be preferred to spiritual food. The Eucharist as well, so long as it is not to our condemnation and without pang of conscience, is always to be received, so that we can hear the Psalmist saying: *Taste and see how good the Lord is (Ps. 33:9)*, and sing with him: *My heart hath brought forth a good word (Ps.*

> *44:1)*. But neither do I affirm that we should fast on feast days, nor that we should eliminate the established festivities of the fifty days of Paschaltide. Rather, let each region abound in its own sense, and diligently examine the precepts of our forebears and the Apostolic laws.[26]

The first thing we should note in this passage is that St. Jerome recognizes that not all ecclesiastical traditions are of the same value; although in general the customs handed down to us from previous generations are to be observed, if and when they are judged to hinder the Faith, they should be laid aside. We shall encounter examples of such traditions further on.

The next thing to be observed is that Jerome favors fasting whenever possible—his zeal is such that he would be happy to fast even at times when Church custom prohibits it, such as Sundays, feast days, and the fifty days of Paschaltide! To justify this zeal he points to the example of St. Paul, who fasted during Paschaltide as well as on Sunday. He clarifies that he does not actually advocate such a course, but the Apostolic precedent helps to reinforce his preferential love for fasting.

Finally, he encourages receiving the Eucharist frequently, even daily, so long as it is done in the proper disposition. Although he does not mention fasting in relation to receiving the Eucharist, he does lay down the principle that carnal food should not be preferred to spiritual food (*carnalis cibus præferri non debuerit spirituali*), which expresses the very logic of the Eucharistic fast. Furthermore, if we examine the Scriptural texts he indicates, in which St. Paul fasted in Paschaltide and on Sunday, we shall see that two of the three references are examples of a proper *Eucharistic* fast, which the Apostle observed even on those festive days.[27] Let us look at these examples.

In Acts 13:1-3, we read that in the Church of Antioch, shortly after Easter, "as they were ministering to the Lord and fasting (Λειτουργούντων δὲ αὐτῶν τῷ Κυρίῳ καὶ νηστευόντων; *ministrantibus autem illis Domino, et jejunantibus*), the Holy Ghost said to them: Separate me Saul and Barnabas, for the work whereunto I have taken them. Then they, fasting and praying and imposing their hands upon them, sent them away." In both the Vulgate and the Greek texts, it is clear that it was a *liturgical,* i.e., Eucharistic, service at which they were assisting, so it makes sense that they were fasting in order to receive the Eucharist. The Mass was especially memorable because in it Sts. Paul and Barnabas were ordained bishops.[28]

The second passage (Acts 20:7-12) is a bit longer:

> And on the first day of the week, when we were assembled to break bread, Paul discoursed with them, being to depart on the morrow. And he continued his speech until midnight. And there were a great number of lamps in the upper chamber (*cœnaculo*) where we were assembled. And a certain young man named Eutychus, sitting on the window, being oppressed with a deep sleep (as Paul was long preaching), by occasion of his sleep fell from the third loft down and was taken up dead. To whom, when Paul had gone down, he laid himself upon him, embracing him, said: Be not troubled, for his soul is in him. Then going up and breaking bread and tasting and having talked a long time to them, until daylight, so

> he departed. And they brought the youth alive and were not a little comforted.

What this passage seems to describe is a Sunday vigil, beginning Saturday evening and culminating with the Eucharistic liturgy at dawn. Most of the night was taken up with preaching, and as Paul was about to depart from Troas, he found it necessary to speak much longer than usual, inducing the young Eutychus to fall asleep—and out of the window to his premature death! St. Paul though, fortified by fasting and prayer, miraculously raised the boy (whose name, incidentally, means *Bona-ventura*, good fortune[29]) from the dead, then proceeded to offer the Eucharist, and broke his fast with Holy Communion. Thus even from Apostolic times, an important way in which the faithful concretely preferred nothing else to the love of Christ in the Eucharist was by fasting.

Another way was for married couples to abstain from marital relations for a determined period of time prior to receiving the Eucharist. St. Paul seems to suggest so himself when writing to the Corinthians: "Defraud not one another, except, perhaps, by consent, for a time, that you may give yourselves to prayer" (1 Cor. 7:5). The implication one could draw from the Apostle's words is that if married couples should abstain for the sake of prayer, they should do so all the more in order to be united to Christ in the Eucharist. But what was merely implied in the Apostle was blatantly spelled out by Jerome.

The occasion for him to do so was the circulation in Rome of a treatise by a certain Jovinian, in which he asserted, among other things, that a virgin was no better than a married woman, and fasting no better than feasting, when done with gratitude. In 393 Jerome's spiritual son, the Roman senator Pammachius, sent the treatise to him in Bethlehem requesting a reply to the numerous dogmatic errors the treatise contained. We can well imagine the ire the treatise aroused in Jerome, given that it attacked the two ascetical practices that were dearest to him—fasting and virginity. Rolling up his sleeves, therefore, he produced his two books against Jovinian, in which he decimated not only Jovinian's arguments, but Jovinian himself.

Other Patristic figures previous to Jerome, Gregory of Nyssa and Ambrose in particular, had written at length arguing for the superiority of virginity over marriage. Jerome repeated their arguments, and admitted to having essentially summarized Ambrose's reasonings. He did so, of course, with a bit more flair. If there was anything he added to Ambrose's logic, it was his interpretation of 1 Corinthians 7:5, which hit Rome like a tidal wave, and angered scores of married men. Pammachius, himself married to one of Jerome's spiritual daughters (Paulina, the daugher of his faithful disciple and benefactor Paula), wrote to him again, suggesting he express his views with a bit more tact. Jerome, though, merely dug in his heels:

> Let married men swell with anger against me for having said: "I ask you, what good is that which hinders prayer: which does not permit me to receive the Body of Christ? When I fulfill the duty of husband, I cannot fulfill that of the continent person." The Apostle commands the same thing in another place—that we pray always (1 Thes. 5:17). "If we are always to pray, the duty of wedlock is never to be kept. For as often as I pay the debt to my wife, I cannot pray." The reason I said this is clear, for I was interpreting that saying of the Apostle: *Do not*

deprive each other, except perchance for a time by mutual consent, that you may devote yourselves to prayer (1 Cor. 7:5). The Apostle Paul says that when we copulate with our wives we cannot pray. If by means of the conjugal act that which is less is hindered, that is, to pray: how much more is that which is greater hindered, that is, to receive the Body of Christ? Peter encourages abstinence: *Lest* our *prayers be impeded (1 Pt. 3:7).* What, I ask, is my sin in this? Of what have I become guilty? What fault have I committed? If the waters that flow are muddy and dark, it is not the canal's fault, but that of the source. Or am I censured for the fact that I dared to add on my own: "What good is that which does not allow me to receive the Body of Christ?" To this I briefly respond. What is greater, to pray, or to receive the Body of Christ? Certainly, to receive the Body of Christ. If through the conjugal act that which is less is hindered, much more is that which is greater hindered. We stated in the same volume that David and his companions were prohibited by the law to eat the loaves of proposition unless they acknowledged themselves to have abstained from women for three days (1 Kings 21), not—to be sure, from prostitutes, which is condemned by the law, but from their wives, to whom they could be lawfully united. Also, the people about to receive the Law on Mount Sinai were commanded to abstain from their wives for three days (Exodus 19). I know that at Rome it is the custom that the faithful always receive Christ's body,[30] something which I neither reprehend nor commend. *Let each one abound in his own understanding (Rom. 14).* But I address myself to the conscience of those who, after intercourse,

> communicate in the same day, and, according to Persius, *purify the night in the stream* (Satyr. 2). Why don't they dare to go to the Martyrs? Why don't they enter the Churches? Is Christ one in public and another at home? What is not allowed in Church is neither allowed at home. Nothing is hidden from God, and even darkness shines for Him. Let each one examine himself, and so draw near to the Body of Christ; not that delaying communion for a day or two makes a Christian any holier, so that what I did not deserve today I shall be worthy of tomorrow or the day after; but that, as I am afflicted with sorrow at not having communicated with the Body of Christ, I might deny myself my wife's embrace, so that I may prefer the love of Christ to the love of my spouse. "It is hard, insufferable," you will say. "What lay person can bear this?" Let him who can bear it bear it: let him who cannot see to it himself. Our concern is not to declare WHAT EACH MAN IS ABLE OR WILLING TO DO, but that which the Scriptures command.[31]

We can picture the tumult this subsequent roar from the lion of Bethlehem must have provoked.

Let us note in passing that Jerome refers to the custom, attested to by other ancient sources as well, of the faithful reserving the Blessed Sacrament (not the Blood, we surmise, but only the consecrated Body) in their homes to be able to communicate daily. Many of us today are understandably taken aback by this, as it seems a lack of respect for something so holy to be kept in a closet along with commonplace items such as books, laundry, or shoes. Rightly so, we might say to ourselves, did the Church do away with this custom. And she did so when she judged the custom to be a hindrance, more than a help, to faith, to use the litmus test provided by St. Jerome. Nevertheless, at one time, perhaps when persecution of the Church was in full vigor, such a measure was not only useful, but maybe even necessary. And in any case, the custom did not entirely vanish, but, rather, was more prudently defined. The Eucharistic Body (not Blood) of Christ was still reserved for the daily reception, and adoration, of the faithful, but in *God's* house, i.e., the Church, where it would be not one object among many, but the very heart of the Church.

Although there are other elements in this last passage that merit closer attention, it is the final part that is most relevant to the question of a worthy reception of the Eucharist: "Let each one examine himself, and so draw near to the Body of Christ; not that delaying communion for a day or two makes a Christian any holier, so that what I did not deserve today I shall be worthy of tomorrow or the day after; but that, as I am afflicted with sorrow at not having communicated with the Body of Christ, I might deny myself my wife's embrace, so that I may prefer the love of Christ to the love of my spouse."

To Jerome's credit, he does make it clear here that marital relations are not wrong in themselves but are legitimate in the eyes of Scripture and the Church. The reason for abstaining from them as a preparation for the Eucharist is to *concretely* prefer Christ's love to the love of one's spouse, something which Christian spouses are obliged to do, at least in principle.[32] Furthermore, the reason someone should abstain from the Eucharist when there is a lack of proper disposition, e.g., when one has not fasted or duly abstained from marital relations, is not to become "holier" or "worthier," but in order to experience the sorrow of being sacramentally separated from

Christ for a time, and to use that sorrow positively as an incentive to refrain from those things which would hinder a worthy reception. And so, the great saint teaches that we receive Christ in the most holy Eucharist "worthily" whenever we concretely prefer nothing else to His love.

If married couples are dismayed by the challenge posed to them by Jerome, they should count their blessings; he was even more exacting with bishops. Commenting on the Apostle's extensive list of qualities to be possessed by a bishop in Titus 1:7-8, Jerome homes in on the last virtue, that a bishop be *continent.* The Greek word St. Paul uses—*sophron*—encompasses a number of virtues, including prudence and chastity, since the deeper meaning of this multifaceted word means to possess a *salutary heart.* Since the Latin text in use at his time had chosen the meaning of prudence instead of chastity, Jerome felt it necessary to clarify the proper meaning of the word in the context of Titus 1:8—and a few other things while he was at it:

> A bishop should also be chaste, which the Greeks term σώφρονα *(sóphrona)*: and which the Latin interpreter, deceived by the double meaning of the word, rendered *prudent,* rather than *chaste.* But if lay people are commanded to abstain from relations with their wives for the sake of prayer, what should we say about a bishop, who for his own sins and those of the people daily offers the unblemished sacrifices to God? Let us read again the books of Kings, and we shall find the priest Abimelech unwilling to give the show bread to David and his servants until he verified that the servants had been unpolluted by woman: and not, to be sure, by an unfamiliar woman, but by their wives (1 Kings 11). And unless he

> heard them affirm themselves to have abstained from marital relations for two days beforehand, he would not have conceded to give them the loaves which he had previously denied them. Such a gap exists between the show bread and the body of Christ as that which exists between bodies and their shadows, the truth and its image, the types of future realities and the realities themselves. To be sure, just as meekness, patience, sobriety, moderation, absence of profit, hospitality and benignity should all be outstanding in a bishop, and excelling that of lay people: so also chastity and modesty are properly priestly, so that he who is about [to] consecrate the body of Christ may have a mind unimpeded not only by impure works, but also by wandering eyes and wayward thoughs.[33]

In order to celebrate the most holy Eucharist daily, a bishop, says Jerome, must have a purity that goes well beyond that of married persons; not only must he abstain from marital relations every time he offers Mass (which, effectively, entails perpetual celibacy), but his very mind should be untroubled by any impure or improper thought when standing at the altar. It is only right, therefore, that the Eucharistic ritual itself, and everything pertaining to it, should be clothed in sacred and otherworldly vestment, to help the bishop be estranged from all that is worldly, and thus to lift up his heart on high. Consequently, in a letter to Theophilus, archbishop of Alexandria, from the year 405, St. Jerome praises the bishop's recent catechesis regarding the veneration due to the items used in sacred worship:

We marveled at the benefit for all the Churches contained in your treatise, that by the evidence of the Scriptures, those who lack knowledge may learn how great the reverence should be with which we receive the Consecrated things, and zealously serve in the ministry at the altar of Christ; and how the sacred chalices and holy veils, and other items which pertain to the veneration of the Lord's Passion, are not to be regarded as superfluous and lacking meaning and empty of holiness; but rather, on account of their close association with the Body and Blood of the Lord are to be treated with the same august veneration as are His Body and Blood.[34]

Chapter 3

Jerome's Early Life and Monastic Vocation

Let us now turn our attention to the particular way in which St. Jerome lived the mystery of the priesthood. This can suitably be done by giving a history of his life *vis-à-vis* the priesthood.

St. Jerome, or, as his full name reads, Eusebius Hieronymus, was born around the year 347 A.D. in Stridon, the exact location of which is a matter of debate among scholars, but it is reasonable to assume it was somewhere on the northern Adriatic coast, not too distant from Aquileia. His father and mother, both pious Catholics, sent him to Rome to complete his studies in 363. Early in his student days in the Eternal City, conspicuous home to both sinner and saint, he fell into temptation and compromised his integrity.[35] Thanks to the positive influence of his friend Bonosus, he found his way back to a life of Christian virtue. Later in life he would recall how on Sundays, with these friends, he would explore the Roman catacombs and venerate the tombs of the Apostles and martyrs.[36] Jerome was eventually baptized by Pope Liberius in 366 at age 19, and from thenceforward tried to live out his Christian faith in earnest. Nevertheless, he never ceased to bewail the sins of his youth.[37]

Upon completing his studies, he traveled with his friend Bonosus to Gaul, spending the bulk of his time in Trier. Here Jerome copied out a commentary on the Psalms, and some other works by St. Hilary of Poitiers, that he would integrate into his growing personal library.[38] It was also in Trier that the monastic ideal first captured his heart, and, consequently, he resolved to give himself entirely to a life serving and worshiping Jesus Christ.[39] We presume this meant as a monk, since it was a monastic form of life he eventually adopted in a community of ascetics near Aquileia, on the Adriatic coast, upon his return from Gaul around the year 370.

The monastic settlement in Aquileia was not exactly a cenobium, but rather a loose-knit community in which the individual members lived the ascetic life in the idiorhythmic manner then typical of Italian monasticism. Along with Rufinus of Aquileia, Heliodorus of Altinum[40], and the priests Innocent and Evagrius of Antioch, St. Jerome and Bonosus tried to give concrete expression to their longing to be monks. Closely associated to this group was the community of the priest Chromatius and his brother Eusebius and Jovinum, to whom Jerome would write a letter at the outset of his eremitical experience in Syria (*Letter 8*). Three years later, however, we see Jerome's ascetic community abruptly disbanded, and each one make his way for the desired homeland of monasticism: the East.[41] While Rufinus went to Egypt to see the desert fathers in person and Heliodorus sailed straight for the holy places in Palestine, Jerome gradually made his way down to Antioch via Thrace (north of Greece) and Asia Minor.

He arrived quite sick in Antioch, sticken by the summer heat, and was grateful to see and be received by his old friend, the priest Evagrius, with whom he had lived the ascetic life in

Aquileia.[42] Evagrius patiently nursed him back to health, reading to him, from time to time, various treatises he had written. Though Evagrius's native city was Antioch, it seems his parents had settled there as Italian expatriates, with the result that Evagrius was equally fluent in Latin and Greek. It seems he befriended St. Eusebius of Vercelli on one of the bishop's visits to Antioch during his exile in the East, and St. Basil relates that Evagrius accompanied the renowned confessor back to Rome and other parts of Italy upon his return to the West.[43] It was, therefore, probably under the aegis of St. Eusebius that Evagrius established connections with the prominent ecclesiastical and political figures of his day, such as Pope Damasus and the Emperor Valentinian,[44] and being a priest of Antioch, he certainly knew the ecclesiastical hierarchy of that city well, eventually becoming a bishop there himself. Like Jerome, he too was a man of letters, eventually producing the definitive Latin translation of Athanasius's *Vita Antonii*.[45]

Given that Evagrius knew the area around Antioch well, it was probably he who first took Jerome to meet Theodosius and the other hermits in the neighboring desert of Chalcis. To them Jerome would address his *Letter 2*, expressing his uncontainable admiration for the example of monastic life he had seen there, while humbly acknowledging that he wasn't quite ready yet to abandon everything to go there; he, consequently, begged them for their prayers to help move his sluggish will into action.[46] Perhaps it was with Evagrius, too, that while visiting that vast desert he met the old monk Malchus, whose heart-rending story he would later recount.

Before the end of his stay in Antioch, he would have the joy of seeing Heliodorus, who visited him and Evagrius in Antioch after leaving Palestine. To Heliodorus he would confide his happy intention to return to the desert of Chalcis, there to remain as long as God desired. Heliodorus seems to have been captured by the same ideal, and asked him to write to him as soon as he had established himself there, so that he could join him.

He did so not long after settling in the desert. One of the most famous letters from this period (*Letter 14*) is addressed to Heliodorus. It is an over-the-top attempt to persuade him to become a monk and join him in the desert, as, indeed, was Heliodorus's intention when they had last seen each other. Alas, for poor Jerome, Heliodorus ultimately discerned a call to the priesthood, eventually becoming the bishop of his native Altinum. The letter and its theme, however, won many devotees who even memorized its contents, such was the radical urgency with which it called souls to abandon everything to follow Christ.[47] Decades later, when Jerome was no longer able to perform the mortifications he praised so much in his youth, he would write to Heliodorus's nephew, the saintly priest Nepotianus (*Letter 52*), and, as a veteran monk, recall the ardent lines he once wrote as a novice:

> When I was coming of age, nay practically still yet a boy, and would curb the initial urges of wanton youth with the desert's austerity, to your uncle, devout Heliodorus, I wrote an exhortative letter abounding in tears and complaints, which, in addition, displayed the affection of his forsaken companion. But in that work, on account of our age at that time we amused ourselves, and, still aflame with the studies and doctrines of orators, sketched out that piece with our scholarly best. Now, with a head of gray hair, and a forehead furrowed with wrinkles, and

> dewlaps like those of an ox sagging down from our chin, *Our cooled-off blood forms a wall round our heart (Virgil. Georg. Lib. 2)*. Therefore, elsewhere the same Poet sings: *Old age robs you of everything, even your wits.* And a little further: *Now I've forgotten so many songs, and even my voice escapes me.* But lest we be seen to collect from pagan writings alone, consider the hidden realites of the sacred books. David at seventy years of age, though once a fiery warrior, with the onset of frigid old age couldn't keep himself warm. Therefore from every end of Israel a maiden is sought—Abisag the Sumamite—who would sleep near the king, to keep his elderly body warm (3 Kings 1).[48]

And in what remains of that enchanting *captatio benevolentiæ*, happily preserved for us as a homily for Matins for the VII Sunday after Pentecost, St. Jerome explains that this Abisag, at once both wife and virgin, represents wisdom—*sapientia*—the virtue which outlives all ascetic labors, and in old age is the loving consort of every man who faithfully pondered God's law in his youth. This playful introduction to his letter to Nepotianus, moreover, reveals that, though the sting of his satirical wit never spared others, as he grew older, he did reserve some of the finer expressions of it for himself.

But let us get back to the letter the *young* Jerome wrote to Heliodorus. It seems Jerome perceived that Heliodorus's delay in joining him in the desert was due to a possible call to the clerical, as opposed to the monastic, state. Even though some of the first monks in Egypt (e.g., Macarius the Great and Moses the Robber) had been called to unite both states of life in themselves in order to provide for the sacramental needs of the other monks, such instances were the exception, not the rule. Indeed, many of the giants of the desert—Anthony, Arsenius, and Pachomius for example, were not priests, and in early monasticism, the priesthood, with the sublime honor, power, and rank it entailed, was part of the *omnia* renounced by the monks.

This was due to many reasons, but we shall try to enumerate at least three. First of all, because the priesthood compromised the monk's search for God in solitude and silent prayer by imposing on him the duty of caring for souls. This does not mean, however, that the unordained monks did not care for souls; on the contrary, many of them were first-rate spiritual directors, and they took very seriously their call to be spiritual fathers to souls, above all through their prayer. Such spiritual paternity, however, was conducted in a way that was harmonius with their callings as monks, and, though constant, was sublimely sponateous and gratuitous, flowing as it did from the only duty that bound them—that of charity. Secondly, the priesthood was generally avoided by monks because the potential power the priestly rank offered provided temptations to envy, a passion that was a notorious destroyer of communities as well as individual souls. Finally, this renunciation was due to the loftiness of the priestly rank, which made the monk's search for humility, compunction, and self-abasement all the more difficult, as it provided a temptation to pride. And, in this connection, it must also be stated that many monks were so convinced of their utter unworthiness to exercise the office that they would simply never entertain the possibility of being ordained, and would make every effort to renounce it should it be offered, or would not exercise the office at all should it be forced upon them.

Let us look at some examples from the desert. The most illustrious of all is perhaps that of St. Pachomius, the founder of cenobitic monasticism:

> After his appointment as archbishop of Alexandria, Apa Athanasius came south to the Thebaid with the intention of proceeding as far as Aswan to give comfort to the holy Churches. When our father Pachomius saw him with an escort of bishops walking before him, he also took the brothers and escorted him a long way. They chanted psalms while escorting him until they brought him inside the monastery, where he prayed in their assembly room and in all their cells. Apa Sarapion, bishop of Nitentori, grasped the archbishop's hand, and kissed it, and said, "I beg Your Piety to ordain to the priesthood Pachomius, the father of the monks, so that he should be set over all the monks in my diocese, for he is a man of God. Alas! he refuses to obey me in this matter." At once Pachomius disappeared into the midst of the crowd so as not to be discovered. When the archbishop had seated himself, as did the great crowd that was with him, he opened his mouth to speak and said to Sarapion, "Indeed I have learned about the renown of the faith of this man Apa Pachomius of whom you speak to me, since I have been at Alexandria and even before my consecration." Then he rose, prayed, and said to [Pachomius'] sons, "Greet your father and say to him, 'So, you hid from us, fleeing from that which leads to jealousy, discord, and envy, and you chose for yourself that which is better and which will always abide in Christ! Our Lord, therefore, will accede to your wish. So now, since you have fled before vain

> and temporary grandeur, not only do I wish for you that that may not happen to you, but I will always stretch my hands toward the Most High that such a thing may never happen to you, and that never, never may you have a rank. Nevertheless, if by God's will we come back to you, may we deserve to see your honorable Piety!'" Then at once he left them and went on south, accompanied by a number of bishops and an immense crowd with lamps, candles, and countless censers. After the archbishop had gone away our father Pachomius came out of the place where he had been hiding.[49]

St. Athanasius, who knew Anthony so well, hoped also to befriend Pachomius, but, at least on this occasion, it was not to be so. Perhaps that is why he was so adamant in his very audible prayer that Pachomius would never have a rank—that was probably the only way Pachomius would feel secure meeting the saintly Archbishop! The first words he addresses to Pachomius, however, are clear in their assessment that Pachomius, in company with Mary at the feet of the Lord, had chosen the better part: "So, you hid from us, fleeing from that which leads to jealousy, discord, and envy, and you chose for yourself that which is better and which will always abide in Christ!"

Some monks, however, did not have Pachomius's good fortune, and were compelled to be priests against their will. In the most peaceful of cases, the monk in question saw that it was God's will for him and surrendered. This is what happened to a monk named Isaac:

> One day they came to make Abba Isaac a priest. Hearing this, he ran away to Egypt. He went into a field and hid

> himself in the midst of the hay. So the clergy went after him in pursuit. Reaching the same field, they stopped there to rest a little, for it was night. They unharnessed the ass to let it graze. The ass went close to the old man, so, when dawn came and they looked for her, they found Abba Isaac too, which filled them with astonishment. They wanted to bind him, but he did not allow it, saying, "I will not run away again. For it is the will of God, and wherever I flee, I find that."[50]

Abba Theodore of Pherme, a monk of Scetis, wasn't able to avoid deaconate ordination, but he refused to serve in the Liturgy. In order to be faithful to his resolution, and in order to avoid the higher office of the priesthood, he had to be ready to abandon his monastic dwelling and go somewhere else:

> It was said about him that, though he was made a deacon at Scetis, he refused to exercise the office and fled to many places from it. Each time the old men brought him back to Scetis, saying, "Do not leave your deaconate." Abba Theodore said to them, "Let me pray God that he may tell me for certain whether I ought to take my part in the liturgy." Then he prayed God in this manner, "If it is your will that I should stand in this place, make me certain of it." Then appeared to him a column of fire, reaching from earth to heaven, and a voice said to him, "If you can become like this pillar, go, be a deacon." On hearing this he decided never to accept the office. When he went to church the brethren bowed before him saying, "If you do not wish to be deacon, at least hold the

> chalice." But he refused, saying, "If you do not leave me alone, I shall leave this place." So they left him in peace.[51]

It seems that the ultimate reason Abba Theodore refused the priesthood was his sense of unworthiness, strongly reinforced by the vision he had of the column of fire and its consequent explanation: *If you can become like this pillar, go, be a deacon*. Theodore, faithful to his own sense of self-knowledge, couldn't thus accept the priestly ministry in good conscience. Abba Matoes, as the following story relates, behaved similarly after he was forcibly ordained to the priesthood against his will:

> One day Abba Matoes went to Rhaithou, in the region of Magdolos. A brother went with him, and the bishop seized the old man and made him a priest. While they were eating together the bishop said, "Forgive me, abba; I know you did not want it but it was in order that I might be blessed by you that I dared to do it." The old man said humbly to him, "I did not wish it, to be sure; but what really troubles me is that I must be separated from the brother who is with me and I am not able to keep on saying the prayers quite alone." The bishop said to him, "If you know that he is worthy, I will ordain him too." Abba Matoes said, "I do not know if he is worthy of it; I know only one thing, that he is better than I." So the bishop ordained him also. Both of them died without having approached the sanctuary to make the offering. The old man used to say, "I have confidence in God that I shall not suffer great condemnation through the laying on of hands since I do not make the offering.

> For the laying on of hands is for those who are without reproach."[52]

One of the most striking things about this anecdote is the motivation the bishop gives for ordaining Matoes: "Forgive me, abba; I know you did not want it but it was in order that I might be blessed by you that I dared to do it": the sacrament of priesthood was conferred merely so that the bishop could get a blessing from the monk! It is also interesting to note the rule in the desert at that time: Matoes alludes to the fact that ordained monks could not dwell together with non-ordained monks. It is a detail of profound meaning because it recognizes the full import of the sacrament. The fact that Matoes did not want the priesthood, or that he chose not to exercise it, did not mean he wasn't a priest. He was a priest, and had to live in a way that respected the truth of who and what he was: a man who carried the priestly character in his soul, according to the words of Scripture: "Thou art a priest for ever according to the order of Melchisedech" (Heb. 7:17; Ps. 109:4). Fortunately for him, his fellow monk was likewise ordained, so that they did not have to be separated from each other.

It is hoped that the few examples we have just seen will help us understand the complex approach the early monks had toward the priesthood. Returning now to young St. Jerome in the desert, we can say that the attitude he had toward the priesthood was very similar to, and most likely influenced by, theirs. And it was this attitude he forcefully communicated to Heliodorus in *Letter 14*:

> 8. But displaced from this order (of monks), you will appeal to the Clerics. Shall I dare to say something

about these, who without doubt dwell in their cities?[1] Far be it from me to say something disparaging about them, for, succeding to the grade of the Apostles, they consecrate THE BODY OF CHRIST with holy words; thanks to them we also are made Christians. They possess the keys of the kingdom of heaven, and in some way judge us before the day of judgment. They safeguard the Lord's bride with sober chastity. The objective, however, of Monks, is different from that Clerics, as I intimated earlier. Clerics feed the sheep: I am fed. They live from the altar: but mine is the fate of the barren tree, to whose base the ax is laid, if I fail to bring a gift to the altar. And I cannot allege poverty as an excuse, when in the Gospel the Lord praised the old widow, who threw into the treasury the only two pennies she had (Luke 21:24). I am not allowed to sit before a priest: to him, though, belongs the power to hand me over to Satan, should I sin, unto the destruction of my flesh, so that my spirit may be saved (1 Cor. 5:5). And in the old Law whoever did not obey the priests was either placed outside the camp or stoned by the people; or, with his neck to the sword exposed, would atone for his scorn with his own blood (Deut. 17:12). Now, indeed, the disobedient man is cut off by the edge of a spiritual sword: or, cast out of the Church, is mangled by the merciless mouth of demons. But if your brethren's pious flattery entice even you to the priestly Order, we shall rejoice at your promotion, but fear your fall.

---

1 As opposed to voluntary exile, which was customary for monks at that time, and about which Jerome had just finished speaking.

He who desires the Episcopacy desires a good work. These words we know well: but do not forget that which follows: *however such a one should be without reproach, the husband of one wife, sober, chaste, prudent, decorous, hospitable, docile, not given to wine, not violent, but modest (1 Tim. 3).* And having listed the other qualities that flow from these, he attaches no less assiduousness to those in the third degree of the priesthood, saying: *Deacons similarly should be chaste: not duplicitous, not given over to wine, not eager for deceitful gain, holding fast to the ministry of faith in a pure conscience. And let these be tried first, and only if they are guilty of no crime let them minister.* Woe to that man who, lacking the nuptial raiment, enters into the wedding feast. There is nothing left for him but to hear straightway: *Friend, how did you get in here?* And he will be speechless, while the servants will be told: *Take him, and binding his hands and feet, throw him into the outer darkness, where there is wailing and gnashing of teeth (Matt. 22:12-13).* Woe to him who wraps the talent he received in a head band, and while the rest are earning profit, he saves nothing beyond that which he received. In that very place he shall be anguished by the outcry of his angry Lord: *Wicked servant, why did you not deposit my money at the bank; so that upon returning I should withdraw it with interest (Matt. 35:16-17)?* That is, you could have laid at the altar that which you were not able to bear. While you, a worthless businessman, hold back your money, you have idly occupied the post in which someone else could have doubled that money. For which reason, just as he who serves well wins for himself a good status: so he who unworthily draws near to the chalice of the Lord shall be answerable for the Body and Blood of the Lord (1 Cor. 11).

9. Not all bishops are bishops. You behold Peter: but consider also Judas. You gaze at Stephen: look also at Nicolaitus, whom the Lord in the Apocalypse by his judgment condemns for having devised such disgraceful and nefarious things, that the heresy of the Nicolaites should arise from him as from its root (cf. Apoc. 2:6,15). Let each man examine himself, and thus draw near. Ecclesiastical rank DOES NOT MAKE a Christian. Cornelius the Centurion while still a pagan is cleansed by gift of the Holy Ghost (Acts 10). Daniel while still a boy judges the elders (Dan. 13): Amos, while picking blackberries from a bush, is suddenly turned into a prophet. David, a shepherd, is chosen to be king (1 King 16). It is the least disciple that Jesus loves most. Sit at the lower place, brother, that when your junior arrives, you may be ordered to move higher (Luke 14). Upon whom will the Lord rest, if not on he who is humble and quiet, and trembles at His words (Is. 66:2)? More is demanded from him to whom much has been entrusted. *The mighty shall be mightily tormented* (Wis. 6:7). And let no man commend himself for mere bodily chastity, when men shall have to give answer in the day of judgement for every idle word they have uttered (Matt. 12:5), and even an insult towards a brother amounts to a crime of homicide. It is no easy thing to hold the place of Paul, to have the rank of Peter, both reigning now with Christ, unless, perchance, an angel come to tear the veil of your temple (Matt. 27:51), and move your candlestick from its place (Apoc. 2:5). He who is about to build a tower computes

> well the cost of the work that awaits him (Luke 14:28). Salt deprived of its taste is good for nothing but to be thrown out, to be trodden over by swine. If a Monk falls, the priest will pray for him. But for the fall of a Priest, who shall pray?[53]

In this impressive passage, Jerome, as he would later acknowledge, thoroughly employs the rhetorical skills he learned while a student. Furthermore, at such a young age, he shows himself to have an excellent command of the Scriptures, and he weaves his arguments entirely from them. Let us try to summarize these arguments.

To begin with, the clergy have an *active* role in the sanctification of the faithful, which consists in the administration of the sacraments ("they consecrate THE BODY OF CHRIST with holy words . . . clerics feed the sheep") and in the responsibility of judging ("They possess the keys of the kingdom of heaven, and in some way judge us before the day of judgment") and enforcing discipline among the lay members of the Church ("to him, though, belongs the power to hand me over to Satan, should I sin, unto the destruction of my flesh, so that my spirit may be saved"). The monk, though having in common with the clergy a total commitment to serving Christ—indeed, he makes a renunciation of the world for this end that goes well beyond that of the secular clergy—he participates, nevertheless, with the laity in the *passive* role of sanctification, which primarily consists in receiving the sacraments ("thanks to them we also are made Christians . . . I am fed"), but also entails submission to the judicial and disciplinary authority of the hierarchy ("now, indeed, the disobedient man is cut off by the edge of a spiritual sword: or, cast out of the Church, is mangled by the merciless mouth of demons").

The monk, thus, bears a weighty responsibility. Like the widow who gave all she had, he must make a complete gift of himself to God at the altar, reserving nothing for himself. His renunciation must exceed that of the clergy in poverty, chastity and, above all, humble obedience, and he must remember that ecclesiastical rank *does not* make a Christian, but, rather, faith, hope, charity, and the grace of the Holy Spirit, who, as Scripture bears witness, lavishes His charisms on the non-ordained members of the Church just as much, if not more, than on the hierarchy.

But the responsibility of the clergy is the weightiest of all. Since the cleric, above all the bishop, has the duty of leading the faithful to God, not only must his life be without reproach, he must labor assiduously at his task in order to obtain a fruitful harvest for the Lord. Failure in his call to holiness (which, Jerome underlines, should far exceed that of the laity) amounts to entering the wedding feast without the nuptial garment; failure in his duty of diligent and unceasing labor for the sanctification of souls amounts to hiding the talent, i.e., the episcopal office, which he received from the Lord, or to idly occupying an office in which someone else could have obtained a far greater return of sanctification. It would have been better for him to humbly place at the foot of the altar that which he was not able to bear, i.e., he should have ceased exercising the clerical office in order to make room for more suitable ministers. A failure in either amounts to a "fall," and, thus, to receiving the Eucharist unworthily and being answerable for the Body and Blood of the Lord.

We can surmise this letter had quite an impact on the young Heliodorus. Subsequent history shows that he remained a devout and diligent pastor to the end, thanks, it seems at least in part, to the principles enunciated by Jerome, since years later his nephew, the priest Nepotianus, would ask Jerome to outline for him the duties of a priest, which he did in the above-mentioned *Letter 52*.

But what about Jerome himself? It seems from his words in *Letter 14* that he was quite sure of his monastic identity, and, therefore, would never accept priestly ordination. As we shall see, his ideals would be compromised somewhat, yet he would always be true to the fundamental principles he laid down in this important letter.

Aside from writing letters to his friends in order to mitigate the harsh solitude into which he had plunged himself, Jerome also visited the neighboring hermits and received their visits in return. By them he would be initiated into the vibrant oral tradition which handed down the lives and miracles of the great monks, including that of St. Paul, the first hermit, whose biography Jerome would soon write. His friend, Evagrius of Antioch, also came to see him often, and not only supplied him with basic necessities but, more importantly, served as his postal carrier, delivering and dispatching for him not only letters, but the desired food of his soul—manuscripts.[54] One of his most generous suppliers of manuscripts was an elderly man named Paul from the town of Concordia, near Aquileia, who was in his hundredth year. As a sign of gratitude for his generosity, Jerome dedicated to Paul his recently composed *Life of St. Paul the First Hermit*, reassuring his elderly benefactor that he was not that old after all—in comparison with St. Paul the hermit, that is, who lived to be one hundred and thirteen.[55]

In *The Life of St. Paul the First Hermit,* St. Jerome held up for himself, and for the Church at large, an enduring example of the humility, simplicity and goodness that emanate from a life fully centered on the worship of God. As Jerome was still a young hermit, warring with the vices of his former life, he probably felt a long way from the sanctity of that first Christian hermit. We can gather so much by the way he brings his short account to a close, for Jerome asks his readers to remember him in their prayers, so that the Lord will bless him with Paul's meritorious poverty, rather than the reprehensible wealth of kings, and refers to himself as *Hieronymi peccatoris,* i.e., Jerome the sinner.[56] In contradistinction to the peace achieved by Paul at the end of his long life, Jerome has left us a vivid account (made famous in countless works of art) of the intense battle which he, like Christ before him, had to face at the outset of his ascetic struggles in the wilderness:

> O how often, when established in my hermitage, and dwelling in that vast seclusion, which, ablaze with the sun's rays, provides a rugged place for monks to live, I thought myself to be amidst the pleasures which abound in Rome. I sat alone, for I was filled with bitterness; my unsightly members clothed in sackcloth shuddered, and scaly skin incased my sunburnt filthy flesh. Each day was filled with tears and groans, and when a looming sleepiness would overwhelm me, I, who battled sleep, would thump onto the earth the naked bones which scarcely clung to it. Concerning food and drink I do not speak, since even utterly infirm monks drink cold water, and to be given something cooked is an extravagance. I, who so lived, therefore, and who, because of fear of

> hell, condemned myself to such a prison, and had for my companions only scorpions and beasts, would often find myself amidst a crowd of dancing girls. My face was pale from fasting, then in a frigid body, my mind in its concupiscence would burn, and nothing save the fires of desire would boil a man already dead before his actual death. Thus, bereft of all assistance, I'd lay prostrate at the feet of Jesus, to bathe them with my tears and dry them with my hair: and by my weekly fasts would conquer my rebellious flesh. I feel no shame to openly admit the misery of my unhappy state; I, on the contrary, regret that I am not now what then I was. I remember calling out non-stop from dawn to dusk, and would not cease inflincting bruises on my breast until tranquility, at the Lord's rebuke, would reappear. I feared my very cell, moreover, as if it were aware of all my thoughts, and both angry with myself and stern, I'd penetrate alone into the desert. If in any place I spotted caverns in the valleys, rough mountaintops, or jagged cliffs, there I'd make my place for prayer, there I'd drag the penitentiary of my poor flesh: and, calling on the Lord Himself to be my witness, after copious tears, after keeping my eyes fixed on heaven, I'd sometimes see myself surrounded by Angelic hosts, and happily rejoicing would sing forth: *Close behind thee shall we run, amidst the fragrance of thy ointments (Cant. 1:3).*[57]

Even more significant than the victories over concupiscence which we see depicted in the previous passage was Jerome's heroic break with the pagan literature he loved so much, a love which can be gleaned in *The Life of St. Paul the First Hermit,* which contains not a few allusions to pagan literature. This literary pleasure did not seem problematic to Jerome at the beginning of his monastic life, but gradually he began to feel a prick of conscience about dedicating so much time to literature from which Christ was completely absent. His old habits, nevertheless, were deeply entrenched and he was not able to let go of his cherished pagan authors, above all Virgil and Cicero. A conflict, therefore, started brewing in his heart that would eventually erupt into a distressing dream which befell him during Lent one year amidst a crippling fever:

> Many years ago, when, for the Kingdom of Heaven, I severed myself from parents, sister, relatives—and what was yet more difficult—my routine fare of finer foods, and journeyed towards Jerusalem to offer service in Christ's army, I simply could not do without the library which I had copied out with utmost care and toil during my student days in Rome. Thus I, a wretch, would fast, and afterwards read Cicero. After repeated all-night vigils, after the tears which memory of my former sins would draw out of my deepest core, I'd take up Plautus in my hands. If every now and then I'd come back to myself and start to read the Prophets, their unpolished discourse made me shudder, and since I could not see the light with my blind eyes, I thought this was the sun's fault, not my eyes'. While the ancient serpent thus made sport of me, about mid-Lent, a marrow-piercing fever invaded my exhausted body, and utterly deprived of rest, my miserable limbs were so consumed, that—something unbelievable to say—they scarcely clung unto my bones. In the meantime, the funeral was being planned, and as

all of my body was now growing cold, the spirit's vital warmth would only pulsate in my tepid heart alone. When, suddenly, snatched up in spirit, I am hauled to the tribunal of the judge, where such brightness, such dazzling splendor radiated from those standing round, that, prostrate on the ground, I dared not raise my sight. When asked about what teaching I adopted in my life, I answered that I was a Christian. Then he who at the court presided said: You lie! You are no Christian, but a Ciceronian, for where your treasure is, there also is your heart (Matt. 6:21). There and then I found myself bereft of speech, and amidst the thrashings (for he charged me to be whipped), I suffered at the pangs of conscience all the more, turning over in myself that verse: "In hell, however, who shall praise Thee?" (Ps. 6:6). I started to cry out, and wailing said: "Have mercy on me, Lord, have mercy," the sound of which resounded through the beatings. At length, those gathered round fell prostrate at the judge's knees, beseeching him grant clemency to youthful age, and accord a place of penance to my erring custom, but promise to inflict grim torments, should I again read pagan authors. Trapped as I was in such a dreadful moment, I longed to promise greater things, and began to swear in solemn fashion; and appealing to His name declared, "Lord if ever I read worldly books again, I have denied Thee." Released amidst these phrases of my sacred oath, I come back to this world; and with all watching in amazement, I open eyes suffused with such a flood of tears, that from my woe I'd kindle faith even in skeptics. And truly that was neither stupor, nor a chain of empty dreams, by which we often are deceived. That

> tribunal, before which I lay prostrate, is my witness, as is the doleful judgment which I feared. May it never come to pass that I should meet with such a questioning again. I confess that I had shoulders bruised and sore, and that once the dream had passed still felt the wounds. Thenceforth I read the sacred tomes with so much zeal, as never I had done with mortal books.[58]

In this celebrated account of the near-death experience that instilled renewed repentance and fear of God in St. Jerome, we observe a milestone conversion/renunciation which, along with several others, would define his deeply Christian identity. Thenceforth, any references he made to pagan authors in his writings were not the result of ongoing reading of such books, but of well-stored verses he had memorized in his youth, just as a bottle filled with water still retains the scent of the first liquid it contained.[59]

However, despite the fact that the pagan authors did not know Christ, Jerome recognized that their writings conveyed, in addition to important philosophical truths, profound literary beauty that had been instrumental in helping him grow closer to God, the author of all beauty. If he could no longer be nourished by that beauty in pagan books, he still needed something to provide it for him. While the prophetic books of the Old Testament conveyed far more truth than the books of pagan philosophers, the Latin translation of those books to which he had access, the *Vetus Latina*, offered him a language that he found rough and unpolished, and could in not compare to the eloquence of his formerly treasured pagan authors. This predicament was probably an important factor in his decision to learn Hebrew so as to read the sacred books of the Old

Testament in the original language, in the hope that there he would find the eloquence and literary beauty for which he so longed.

And he was not confounded in his expectations. After learning Hebrew he would see why the Latin text was so awkward: because it was translated from the Greek by men who might have been eloquent in their own right, but who did not know Hebrew, and consequently, could not read the original. Thus, they were looking at the surface of the reality, not penetrating into its depths, and produced a translation that was like a shabby gown that kept us from beholding the comely figure hidden beneath. But, to one who can behold that lovely form, i.e., to one who can read Hebrew, Jerome would ask: what is more poetic or more singable than the Psalter, with its intricate alternation of meters and rhythms? What is more beautiful than the canticles of Isaiah and Deuteronomy? What is more solemn than Solomon, or more perfect than Job?[60]

But he did not attain such competence in the language of Abraham overnight. It required a formidable commitment, and thus a considerable portion of his time in the desert was dedicated to the study of Hebrew. In its own way, this training constituted an asceticism no less mortifiying than fasting, vigils, or sleeping on the ground, as he would later relate:

> When I was young, and the solitude of the desert walled me in on all sides, I could not endure the allurments of vice and the vehemence of nature, which, though I would quash with frequent fasts, my mind, nonetheless, would still boil with troubling thoughts. In order to tame it, thus, I consigned myself to a certain brother who, from the Jews, came to the faith, so that, after the

> subtlety of Quintilian, the fluent speeches of Cicero, the solemn dignity of Fronto, and the smoothness of Pliny, I should learn anew my letters, and drill myself with words of aspirated harshness. My conscience, and that of they who shared my life then are the witnesses of the great toil that it cost me, of what difficulty I endured, how often I despaired, how often I gave up, then once again, thanks to an eager striving after learning, would start anew. And I thank the Lord that from the bitter seed of study, I now reap luscious fruits.[61]

And with him every Roman Catholic should give thanks as well. For centuries, day in and day out, the Church has benefitted from the toil of that learning, for she integrated the bulk of Jerome's translation of the Scriptures into the Vulgate, her own version—*translatio nostra*—as she would happily say. St. Jerome's rendering of the Scriptures into Latin greatly benefitted, moreover, from his thorough knowledge of, and love for, classical Latin literature. Despite the criticisms that scholars have arrogantly leveled at the Vulgate throughout history (especially in the last century) for its unavoidable human limitations, for those of us who are still nourished by the streams of its charming idiom, how dear Jerome's language is to us. How dry, indeed, would our Advent be without: *Rorate cæli desuper, et nubes pluant justum* (Is. 45)? How plain Epiphany without: *Omnes de Saba venient, aurum et thus deferentes* (Is. 60)? How forlorn the Triduum without: *Quomodo sedet sola civitas* (Lam. 1)? And what triumph would be lacking to Paschaltide without: *Quis est iste, qui venit de Edom* (Is. 63)? It doesn't take long for us to take stock of how indebted we are to Jerome for his labor in the wilderness, for today, we, too, still reap from it the choicest fruits.

Chapter 4

The Antiochian Schism and the End of His Desert Experience

Although Jerome probably intended to remain in the desert for an extended period of time, perhaps his whole life, his eremitical experience soon came to an end. It did so due to a theological controversy that was tearing apart the Church of Antioch, and the East in general; a controversy, furthermore, in which the monks passionately participated. Three of Jerome's letters on this subject have come down to us: two written to Pope Damasus (*Letters 15* and *16*) and one to a certain priest of Chalcis named Mark, who was probably the monk-priest who oversaw the monks in the desert inhabited by Jerome (*Letter 17*). From his letter to Mark the priest, we gather that the neighboring monks repeatedly interrogated Jerome to know where he stood. Despite his best attempts to express his orthodoxy, it seems he had numerous enemies who were not satisfied with his confession. He thus suffered something of an excommunication from them, for they persuaded some brothers who were dwelling near him to abandon him, and barely conceded to him his small patch of wilderness:

> Not one corner of this desert is granted me. Every day my faith is questioned, as if I were reborn deprived of it each day. I make a confession, as they desire, but it fails to satisfy. One thing alone satisfies them, that I leave this place. I now yield, for they tore away from me part of my soul, my dearest brothers. See, they want to leave me, indeed, they are leaving, saying that "it is better to live with the beasts than with Christians like you."[62]

Letters 15 and *16* of Jerome, both written in the year 376, are addressed to Pope Damasus. Although Damasus did not begin his pontificate until the close of 366, at the very end of Jerome's student days in Rome, it is possible that Jerome knew him when he was still a priest, or that Evagrius introduced Jerome to Damasus by means of letter. In any case, Jerome had some acquaintance with the Pontiff. His first letters to him are famous for containing a clear Patristic witness to the Roman primacy. They reinforced some of the basic ideas subsequent Roman Catholicism would hold about the Roman See, such as its universal jurisdiction,[63] its steadfastness in doctrinal purity,[64] and its role as foundation and guarantee of Christian unity.[65] The occasion for Jerome to write them was the heated controversy he was facing in the desert.

The controversy was twofold. First, the See of Antioch had been in schism for fifteen years, since 361, and Jerome was being forced to voice his allegiance to one of the three claimants: Vitalis, Meletius, or Paulinus.[66] As Jerome did not know any of them, he was asking Damasus which of the three was the rightful claimant. Let us try to understand in some degree the unfolding of this terribly messy, though highly significant, episode in Church history.

The historian Socrates relates[67] that when the Arians came to exert a majority rule in and around Antioch, the orthodox bishop of that city, Eustathius, was sent into exile.[68] The Arians then installed Meletius as bishop of Antioch, since they believed him to share their heretical opinions; they were soon proved wrong, however, when hardly thirty days into office Meletius started to preach the orthodox doctrine of Nicaea, which was summed up in the word *homoousios* (of the same substance). He, too, therefore, was sent into exile, and a man of unquestionable Arian persuasion, Euzoius, was made bishop instead. Each of the exiled orthodox bishops however—Meletius as well as Eustathius—had left behind themselves a flock of faithful partisans. The followers of Meletius, which constituted the larger of the two orthodox groups, worshipped in the *old* church of Apostolic origin in the ancient city, which ran along the banks of the Orontes River. St. John Chrysostom grew up in this half of the orthodox community and was eventually ordained a deacon by Meletius. The followers of Eustathius, however, refused to be in communion with Meletius due to his once vague relationship to the Arians, and, under the leadership of the priest Paulinus, worshipped in the new city, which was situated on an island amidst the waters of the Orontes (accessible by five bridges), in a small church which Euzoius kindly conceded to Paulinus on account of the respect he had for him.[69] The orthodox believers in Antioch were thus divided into two camps: that of Meletius and that of Paulinus, who at the time was still a presbyter.

In this period two notable orthodox bishops from the West were exiled to the East on account of their indefatigable defense of St. Athanasius and the creed of Nicaea, Eusebius of Vercelli and Lucifer of Cagliari. In 361 they were both relegated to the Egyptian Thebaid, but at the end of that year their exile came to a close. Before embarking on their return journey to the West, however, they played a significant role in the history of the Antiochian schism. Clearly troubled by the way things were going in Antioch, they resolved to try to help the matter. Eusebius went to Alexandria to participate in an important synod that was to be held in 362 under the presidency of St. Athanasius (himself just returned from exile) in order to resolve the schism of Antioch. Lucifer sent a deacon to represent him at this synod, promising to adhere to its proceedings, then made his way to Antioch to see how he could help the situation personally.[70] Alas, he only made it worse, for while the council was deciding in favor of Meletius, imploring his followers to be reconciled with Paulinus and his adherents, Lucifer, whose sympathies were much more in line with Paulinus (given that Paulinus was generally favored by the Western bishops, and that Athanasius himself would commune with his group when in Antioch[71]), ordained Paulinus a bishop, and thus hardened the schism that was on the point of being healed. When Eusebius of Vercelli, the man Athanasius hand-picked to deliver the proceedings of the Alexandrian synod—the *Tomus ad Antiochenos*[72]—arrived in Antioch, he was thus understandably dismayed by Lucifer's actions.[73] But as he could not undo the ordination, he labored much to bring about a reconciliation between the two groups. This was to no avail, however, for upon the elevation of Julian to the imperial throne, Meletius was called back from exile, and received with great joy by his followers.

In addition to Paulinus's episcopal ordination, a major point of contention that prolonged the schism was a disagreement over theological terminology, and this is the second part of the controversy Jerome faced in the desert and writes about in his letters to Damasus. Let us try to understand something of this complex controversy as well.

The First Ecumenical Council of Nicaea had clarified that the Son was consubstantial, or *homoousios,* with the Father, literally of the same *ousía* or being as the Father. It thus offered the terminology for speaking about the one divine essence shared by the Most Holy Trinity. What the council did not determine was the terminology to be used in order to speak about the three subsisting Persons, and consequently, how to speak about the individual properties that distinguished the three divine Persons from each other.

This lack of doctrinal clarity gave rise to a new word which was being used by both orthodox believers as well as heretics to speak about the three persons: *hypóstasis.* The orthodox believers would use the term to denote the individually subsisting Persons within the Trinity, and thus it was a way to safeguard the unity of the divine Persons. In other words, if one understood *hypóstasis* to mean *person,* one could say that the *hypóstasis* of the Son was distinct from the *hypóstasis* of the Father. The argument for this position was most clearly expressed by St. Basil of Cesarea in his treatise *De Spiritu Sancto* (the teaching of which the Church would eventually make her own in the Second Ecumenical Council of Constantinople of 381), and was summarized in the phrase "one *ousía,* three *hypóstases.*"

Duplicitous heretics of Arian persuasion, however, were using the term ambiguously, and though they gave the impression of using it in an orthodox manner, they actually intended *hypóstasis* to be synonymous with *ousía,* i.e., substance, and consequently destroyed the faith established at Nicaea. They, too, therefore, would say that the *hypóstasis* of the Son was different from the *hypóstasis* of the Father, but as they intended *hypóstasis* to mean *ousía,* they were effectively saying that the substance of the Son is entirely alien from that of the Father. Indeed, as Jerome points out to Damasus, in classical Greek literature *hypóstasis* typically means *ousía;*[74] although the word had also the meaning of person, *prósopon* in Greek, this meaning was just starting to become prominent in those years, and perhaps thanks to this theological controversy. The Alexandrian synod of 362 had recognized that, although *hypóstasis* could be used in an orthodox manner, there were still ambiguities in its use at that time, and thus pleaded the warring factions of Antioch to refrain from using it and limit themselves to the language of Nicaea.[75] This plead was not heeded, however, and the war over the term continued to rage not only in Antioch, but especially in the deserts of Chalcis, eventually compelling Jerome to leave.

Chapter 5

Priestly Ordination and Studies in Antioch and Constantinople, 380-382

When exactly Jerome left the desert is not clear, but it seems to have been in 377 or 378. It is also unknown what he did immediately upon leaving the desert, and especially with whom he resided. During his time in the desert, he probably made many acquaintances and may have had a number of places to settle. But given the strong connection that he had with the priest Evagrius, it seems likely that upon leaving the desert he went to stay with him. Socrates tells us that Evagrius succeeded Paulinus as bishop of his faction of the Church of Antioch;[76]consequently, it was probably he who introduced Jerome to Paulinus. Furthermore, it is possible that Damasus did, in fact, respond to Jerome's letters, and acknowledge that he was in communion with Paulinus.[77]

Once Jerome came to know Paulinus's history, we can imagine he felt spiritually safe with him, for his orthodoxy was beyond dispute. Paulinus was supported, furthermore, by an influential bishop who probably made Jerome's acquaintance for the first time in these years: Epiphanius of Salamis.[78] As Epiphanius's role in Jerome's life was significant, and, moreover, is instrumental in understanding Jerome's relationship to the priesthood, it is fitting to say a word of introduction about him.

St. Epiphanius was born of Christian parents in Eleutheropolis in Palestine in 315.[79] He became a monk at an early age, first in the deserts of Egypt under Abba Hilarion (whose life and miracles, which he learned from Epiphanius, Jerome would later recount), then in a monastery he founded in his native Eleutheropolis, where he served as abbot for some thirty years before becoming the Bishop of Salamis on the island of Cyprus in 367.[80] He kept close bonds with his monastery of Eleutheropolis, however, which seemed to remain under his jurisdiction even after he was made bishop. During the course of his long life, he also kept good relations with the monks in Egypt, something which can be gathered from the seventeen sayings attributed to him in the *Apophthegmata Patrum*, or *Sayings of the Desert Fathers*. Sayings 8-11 show him to be an ascetic who valued erudition and had a special love for the study of the Holy Scriptures, traits which must have particularly endeared the bishop to Jerome:

> He [Epiphanius] also said, "The acquisition of Christian books is necessary for those who can use them. For the mere sight of these books renders us less inclined to sin, and incites us to believe more firmly in righteousness."
>
> He also said, "Reading the Scriptures is a great safeguard against sin."
>
> He also said, "It is a great treachery to salvation to know nothing of the divine law."
>
> He also said, "Ignorance of the Scriptures is a precipice and a deep abyss."[81]

This last saying: "Ignorance of the Scriptures is a precipice and a deep abyss," is reminiscent of what is perhaps the most famous phrase that has come down to us from St. Jerome: *ignoratio Scripturarum, ignoratio Christi est,* i.e., "Ignorance of the Scriptures is ignorance of Christ."[82] Moreover, Epiphanius had little tolerance for heresy, and set himself to eradicate it as soon as it began to appear, an important characteristic of Jerome as well. Given the similarity of mentality that existed among these two men, therefore, we can say that they were at least kindred spirits; moreover, given Epiphanius's long monastic experience, and that he was Jerome's senior by some thirty years, it seems reasonable to infer that he became a sort of spiritual father to Jerome, something we may imagine the young monk desperately needed after his trying times in the desert.

But there was one matter the saintly old bishop saw somewhat differently from Jerome. He represented a strand of desert monasticism, probably the minority, that did not see monasticism and priesthood as mutually exclusive. On the contrary, as his own example bears witness, he thought the two went quite well together, an opinion shared by St. Eusebius of Vercelli, St. Augustine in the West, and St. Basil in the East.[83] Furthermore, as we shall see later in this narrative, capturing and ordaining monks to the priesthood was something of an irresistible passion of his. Incidentally, this helps us to understand the ancient monastic dictum transmitted to us by St. John Cassian—that monks should at all costs avoid both women . . . and bishops![84]

Although we cannot know with certainty, it seems that once Epiphanius had entered his life, Jerome saw the writing on the wall, so to speak, and gathered that in all probability he was not going to avoid priestly ordination. Apart from this supposition, it was clear to him that he was called to, and wholeheartedly wanted to, devote his life to the study and explanation of the Scriptures, and he probably understood that such a call would benefit from the grace and priestly character conferred by the sacrament. And thus, he acquiesced to being ordained a presbyter in the year 379.

However, it would not be Epiphanius who would ordain him, but Paulinus. And it was not Jerome who solicited ordination; rather, it was Paulinus (and perhaps Epiphanius too) who brought up the matter to Jerome. Jerome himself would tell us many years later:

> The bishop Paulinus of blessed memory heard from me, a wretch of a man: "Did I ask you to be ordained? If in conferring the priesthood you do not deprive us of the monastic state, do as it seems best to you. But if by the title of priest you divest me of that on account of which I forsook the world, I hold on to that which I've always had: you have suffered no loss in this ordination."[85]

These words shed great light on the issue. First of all, they indicate that it was Paulinus who took the initiative in ordaining Jerome. We can imagine that from Paulinus's point of view, the reputation Jerome was acquiring as a devout ascetic and erudite teacher of the Scriptures had singled him out as an evident candidate for the priestly office. It should also be kept in mind that one of Paulinus's own priests, Evagrius, knew Jerome well and had probably recommended his friend to the bishop. Furthermore, it makes sense that Paulinus would have wanted to ordain Jerome for the simple reason that a greater number of presbyters under his jurisdiction would have increased his chances of being reckoned the rightful Bishop of Antioch—something everyone in this group, including Epiphanius and Jerome, wanted too.

But Jerome was remarkably astute in maneuvering this situation. Although accepting ordination seemed like the better thing to do because it would benefit his own calling to explain the Scriptures *and* help the orthodox cause in Antioch, nevertheless, he was a monk, and had no doubts about the preeminence of this calling over everything else. Consequently, he needed to protect it, and made his unquestionable attachment to the monastic state a *sine qua non* of priestly ordination. In other words, he would accept ordination, but not at the cost of losing the freedom necessary to preserve his monastic identity. Should Paulinus pressure him to take up a ministry that would threaten this identity, the bishop would find himself short of a priest, or to interpret Jerome's own words, Jerome would carry on as he did before, as if he had never been ordained: *nullum dispendium in ordinatione passus es.*

St. Jerome's priestly ordination was, therefore, something of a paradox: he accepted the priestly state, yet, from the very beginning, expressly renounced all priestly ministry and duties; and, although we cannot know for sure, later events in his life suggest that this renunciation was absolute. He expressly did this, moreover, in order to safeguard the primacy of the monastic state in his life; but we may surmise there were other reasons as well.

One of these reasons was the life of perpetual penance to which he felt called. Although this penitential dimension was already a part of the monastic calling, Jerome felt a particularly personal need to weep, not only for his own sins (especially those of his youth) but for the deep brokenness resulting from Original Sin in general, a brokenness of which he was keenly aware, as can be gleaned from numerous passages in his writings.

One evident reason why he may have chosen to refrain from priestly ministry was in order to dedicate himself to the great labor of his life—to explain the Scriptures, and to hand on to his Latin-speaking brethren the erudition of both the Hebrews and Greeks.[86] He needed, therefore, to acquire that learning himself, both through ongoing personal study and by attending the lectures of distinguished men of learning, both of which demanded a great amount of leisure. While in Antioch he frequently attended the lectures of Apollinaris of Laodicea on Scriptural interpretation, and sought to learn his methods of exegesis while disregarding his erroneous Christology.[87] Soon afterwards, he left Antioch for Constantinople to study under St. Gregory Nazianzen, a bishop of profound intellect, vast learning, refined eloquence, and unquestionable orthodoxy. St. Jerome would happily boast to have had him as his teacher in the Faith on more than one occasion.[88] From both Apollinaris and Gregory Nazianzen, Jerome would come into considerable contact with the teachings and writings of Origen, and thenceforth incorporate the exegetical methods of the Alexandrian master into his own teaching on Scripture.

Origen (185-254), Jerome tells us, was a great man from his birth. His father, Leonidas, died a martyr. Origen himself ran a theological school in Alexandria, continuing the work of his teacher, the priest Clement. He fled from all pleasures to the point that he castrated himself, out of zeal for God, to be sure, but not according to knowledge. He trampled on avarice, knew the Scriptures by heart, and would work himself to a sweat day and night in expounding them. He produced innumerable treatises and commentaries . . . so many that Jerome exclaims, "Who among us is able to read everything he wrote? Who will not marvel at his fervor for the Scriptures?"[89] The man also wrote in very eloquent Greek, and St. Jerome may have found in his writings something comparable to the literary beauty he formerly treasured in the pagan authors. From Jerome's point of view, therefore, it was Origen's love for the Holy Scriptures, his tireless search to understand them and his ability to eloquently expound them that impressed him most, qualities which he also tried to imitate. However, in addition to recognizing Origen's virtues, he also recognized his shortcomings.

Indeed, Origen was gifted with a colossal intellect. In his writings he brought the Gospel face to face with ancient Greek thought and provided the concepts and terminology from Greek philosophy that enabled the many Christian thinkers to better penetrate the content of revelation and explain it to others. As such, his writings formed foundational "textbooks" of Christian theology. Everyone was indebted to him, everyone drew from the abundant fountain of his thought, either directly or indirectly.

But the ultimate principles that emerged from Origen's synthesis of Christianity and Greek philosophy were distinct from, indeed, antithetical to, the content of revelation and the basic principles of orthodox faith. The result was that his writings furnished ample ammunition to both friend *and* foe of the Christian commonwealth. While the orthodox fathers took from Origen whatever they could put at the service of the Gospel, resulting in excellent fruits in Scriptural exegesis and dogmatic and mystical theology, the heterodox were likewise finding in Origen the principles and arguments to further their heretical purposes. The writings of Origen can thus be compared to a great sea, which, in addition to being the source of many blessings, is also a perilous menace that threatens to annihilate whatever stands in its engulfing waves. Like the inhabitants of the Low Countries, always striving against the sea that threatens to submerge them, the Church has always had to protect itself from the errors of the formidable Alexandrian genius. The Church faced the Origenist crisis most intensely during the violent Iconoclastic controversies of the eighth century, a strife from which "the Church in Byzantium has never recovered her inner unity," as one historian has remarked.[90] But she encountered it first in the life-time of St. Jerome—indeed, his very life was bound up with the Origenist controversy.

Jerome was in a decidedly optimistic phase in regard to Origen during the time he spent in the Imperial City, as can be seen by the numerous translations he made of Origen's homilies on the prophets in these years. This favorable attitude to Origen would last for over a decade. Nevertheless, he also showed an independence of thought in relation to his admired mentor, and an ability to state his errors. This is evident in a treatise of Scriptural interpretation, perhaps his first ever, which he wrote on the vision of Isaiah in Isaiah chapter 6. Although he presented the treatise to Pope Damasus shortly after arriving in Rome the following year (it is counted as number 18 of his letters), he composed it when still in Constantinople. Commenting on the words, "I saw the Lord sitting on a lofty and elevated throne; and the house was filled with his glory, and Seraphim stood all around him" (according to the LXX), Jerome states:

> Certain persons before me, both Greek and Latin, expounding this passage have reckoned the Lord sitting upon the throne to be God the Father, and the two Seraphim that stand on either side crying out to be our Lord Jesus Christ and the Holy Ghost. Though they be among the most erudite authorities, I do not assent to their interpretation. IT IS MUCH BETTER to say true things in modest and unadorned speech, than to pronounce false things with great eloquence; this is especially the case in this passage, since in this very Vision, John the Evangelist said it was Christ who was seen, not God the Father. Indeed, when speaking of the unbelief of the Jews he said: *And therefore they could not believe, because Isaias said again: He hath blinded their eyes and hardened their heart, that they should not see with their eyes, nor understand with their heart and be converted: and I should heal them. These things said Isaias, when he saw his glory and spoke of him (Is. 6:9,19; Jn 12:40-41).* In the present volume of Isaiah, therefore, it is commanded by Him who sits on the throne to say: *Hearing, hear and understand not.* But He who commands these things, as the Evangelist understands, is Christ: from this it can now be gathered that the Seraphim cannot be Christ, if it is Christ Himself who is seated.[91]

One of "the most erudite authorities" alluded to in this passage, with whom Jerome did not agree, was Origen. Although Origen's position was problematic theologically because it subordinated the Son and the Holy Spirit to God the Father and thus introduced inequality into the Most Holy Trinity, Jerome does not oppose it on theological grounds, but forms his argument on the unity of Holy Scripture. With his customary and firm Scriptural logic, he asserts that Origen's position is untenable because it disagrees with the interpretation given to the passage by St. John the Evangelist. He thus reads Isaiah in the light of St. John's Gospel, that is to say, the two Testaments in light of each other, as we have seen before. Indeed, he identifies the two Seraphim as signifying the Old and New Testaments, which glorify the Holy Trinity in harmonious unity:

> That which we read in the Old Testament we likewise find in the New: and what is read in the Gospel can be concluded by the authority of the Old Testament; nothing in them is dissonant, nothing is dissimilar. *And they cried out, Holy, Holy, Holy Lord God of Hosts.* In both Testaments the Trinity is proclaimed.[92]

We see that, although Jerome rectified Origen's position, he did not name him explicitly in denouncing his error, but referred to him *tacito nomine,* anonymously, as it were; neither, for that matter, did he name him when making use of the many positive insights he drew from him. Perhaps we can see here a mark of prudence which he learned from St. Gregory Nazianzen, for, by not explicitly naming Origen as the source of the profitable elements in his exegesis, he did not need to associate him with the unprofitable elements he found in the same source. He thus preserved the honor of his teacher by not calling attention to the heterodox elements in his teaching. It was perhaps one of Jerome's greatest *faux pas* to have departed from this path, for once he openly began praising Origen's brilliance, it was just a matter of time before he needed to denounce his unorthodoxy as well.

Chapter 6

Jerome's second period in Rome, 382-385

The Roman Synod

As was mentioned previously, St. Jerome presented the treatise on the vision of Isaiah to Pope Damasus in Rome the following year. Although he may have gone to the Eternal City at the pontiff's request, we have no extant record of such an invitation. Nevertheless, the theory is tenable given the great interest Damasus had in Scriptural exegesis and Jerome's growing prestige as an authority on Scripture. The relationship that had been evolving between the two Church men may very well have led Damasus to request the young scholar's presence in Rome not only to assist him as a *peritus* in Scriptural matters, but, perhaps more importantly, to offer his insights into the troubling situation in Antioch and other problems the Church was facing.[93] Indeed, an important synod had been summoned by Imperial decree for 382,[94] and Jerome arrived in Rome in the Fall of that year, along with his friends and Episcopal patrons Paulinus and Epiphanius, who had been invited to participate in the upcoming synod.

Unfortunately for Paulinus, however, the synod did not resolve the conflicted situation in Antioch. This is understandable because Damasus was being bombarded by both sides, and feared losing the one by siding with the other. St. Basil, before his death in 379, had rallied for Meletius's cause and enlisted the support of the majority of bishops in the East. He may have even won St. Ambrose to his side, which would have made a considerable difference, since Ambrose wielded an unrivaled influence in the ecclesiastical and political matters of the West. Given Damasus's indebtedness to Evagrius of Antioch, however, and the promising collaborative relationship he was beginning to enjoy with St. Jerome, he probably felt inclined to side with Paulinus. In any case, both he and the synod refrained from making a clear decision in the matter, and the Antiochian schism lingered on until 389.

JEROME'S WORK AS PAPAL SECRETARY AND REVISER OF THE LATIN NEW TESTAMENT

After the synod was concluded Epiphanius and Paulinus returned to their Eastern dioceses. Jerome, however, did not return to Antioch with Bishop Paulinus; rather, he stayed on in Rome, presumably at the request of Pope Damasus. Seventeen years later he would write: "Many years ago, when [I was] assisting Damasus, the Bishop of Rome, with Ecclesiastical documents, and would respond to questions from East and West relating to the Synod . . . ."[95] From this it can be gathered that Jerome served Damasus as a sort of secretary in the aftermath of the synod; indeed, he may have had an official function in the very running of the council itself, given his fluency in Latin and Greek. This close collaboration with Pope Damasus was the foundation for the assertion of later hagiographical writings that Jerome was elevated by Damasus to the dignity of a Cardinal, a belief that was canonized in countless paintings that can still be seen today in museums and churches all over the world. If the cardinalate dignity existed in some primitive form at that time, we can be sure that Damasus would have given it to Jerome, but we can also be sure that Jerome would have had no interest in it; one only has to call to mind the terse words he wrote to Heliodorus a decade earlier: "Ecclesiastical dignity DOES NOT MAKE a Christian (*NON FACIT Ecclesiastica dignitas Christianum*)." Indeed, the monk and doctor, whose delight was to fast and study the Scriptures, gloried in nothing but this—to be a Christian.

And it was, after all, Jerome's love for and expertise in the Holy Scriptures that Damasus prized above all. Accordingly, he turned to Jerome with all manner of questions he had about the Scriptures. *Letter 36* of Jerome to Damasus shows him responding to questions on the meaning of the seven-fold punishment to be inflicted on anyone who kills Cain; on why the sacred page states that the Israelites were to return from Egypt in the fourth generation after Abraham, yet in another place in the fifth; and why Isaac, who was a just man, was not able to bless the son he willed to bless, but rather the one he did not want to bless. Two important treatises, furthermore, have come down to us from this time in which Jerome responded at length to some of Damasus's questions: a longer, and very moving, exposition of the parable of the prodigal son (*Letter 21* to Damasus); and a detailed explanation of the Hebrew word "Hosanna" (*Letter 20* to Damasus).

It was fitting that in these early days of his second, and last, Roman sojourn Jerome should write about that acclamation of greeting and praise—Hosanna—which the crowds directed to Our Lord when He entered Jerusalem on Palm Sunday.

Indeed, since the previous year, when first he descended upon the Eternal City flanked by his two illustrious bishop protectors, until the present time, when he was virtually regarded by Pope Damasus as a prophetic oracle, everyone in Rome sang his praises. *Omnium pene judicio dignus summo Sacerdotio decernebar,*[96] he would dejectedly say at the fateful end of his stay in Rome: "By nearly everyone I was considered worthy of the high priesthood," i.e., the papacy. Soon enough, however, the cries of "Hosanna" would become shouts of "Crucify him!" for Jerome too.

This drastic turn of events would begin with one of Jerome's greatest achievements. As Damasus came to know his competence in matters Scriptural, the pontiff decided to entrust to him the colossal task that would remain a singular triumph of his pontificate: a revised and authoritative Latin text of the New Testament.

There were already Latin translations of the Greek New Testament; in fact, there were too many, and there were significant differences among them. Jerome captured the heart of the difficulty when he said: "There are virtually as many versions as there are manuscripts."[97] In some versions, he tells us, there were manifest errors of translation; in others, attempts to correct those errors resulted in even greater inaccuracy; finally, there were "sleeping copyists" who added or changed words somewhat arbitrarily. It commonly happened, furthermore, that in the Gospel of Mark there were abundant passages peculiar to Luke alone, or that in Matthew far more from John and Mark was to be found than from Matthew himself. Many manuscripts offered, consequently, an assortment of elements from the sacred authors.

Of course, this reality, as messy as it seems to us, did not present much of a problem to most folks at that time. For a Church which had lived for centuries under the constant fear of persecution, simply to have access to the Sacred Text was already an inestimable boon. What did it matter if something was attributed to Mark that was actually written by John? Was not the important thing that it ultimately came from Christ Himself? Indeed, to those faithful who had grown old with the version they had been used to since their youth, hearing it was as natural as swallowing their own saliva. To hear a *new* version, even if objectively more faithful to the Greek original, would be considered a sacrilege, and immediately rejected by most people, along with the impious man who dared to tamper with God's word—or at least *their* version of it.

Consequently, Jerome knew what he was in for. His consolation amidst the inevitable animosity he was to undergo was twofold: first, that this was asked of him in obedience by the Church's highest priestly authority, the Pope; and second, the realization that the versions in circulation which varied so much among themselves simply could not reflect the Scriptural truth, something which even the insults he would hear from the people angry at seeing "their" version changed would corroborate. But there would be additional reasons for the envy he would draw from the Roman clergy and populace.

Jerome's Pastoral Involvement with the Consecrated Women on the Aventine

There was a noblewoman, a saintly widow named Marcella,[98] who first heard the "good news" of the monastic charism directly from St. Athanasius himself when he was exiled in

Rome in 340, and received further instruction in the monastic life from Athanasius's successor, Peter, when he was in Rome from 373-374. She alone, of all her contemporaries who learned about the monastic life, started to practice in earnest what she had heard, and essentially converted her home on the Aventine hill to a nunnery. In time, other women in Rome would imitate her example, turning their homes into urban monasteries, and around Marcella herself a choir of widows and virgins eventually formed so as to turn the Aventine into a sort of monastic oasis.[99] But before going deeper into the details of this company of nuns, and St. Jerome's involvement in it, let us first understand Jerome's own monastic existence in Rome.

As he was intent to preserve the monastic identity he formed during his time in the desert, we can imagine that, except for his work at the papal curia, he rarely left his monastic dwelling. We know that at some point during the time he spent in Rome, a monk-priest named Vincent, whom he had befriended during his student days in Constantinople, came to join him in Rome.[100] A monk from Cremona named Eusebius made Jerome's acquaintance at this time and, it seems, shared a common monastic life with him and Vincent. Finally, Jerome invited his younger brother Paulinian to join them. This group of four ascetics, then, constituted a core group that would share the monastic life for many years to come.[101]

As it was Jerome's custom to abstain from meat and follow the fasts common to the monastic state at that time, we can imagine his companions in the common life did the same. Essentially, this meant perpetual abstention from meat and taking one meal daily. This meal was customarily taken after the ninth hour for most of the year, but in Lent was taken after Vespers, and in Paschaltide at midday.[102] They would have likewise followed the monastic manner of praying the Divine Office throughout the day and night. At the time this consisted of the Office of the Dawn (later known as Lauds) then Terce, Sext, None, Vespers, grace before and after the daily meal, and two or three segments of prayer during the course of the night.[103] Beyond these basic practices of the ascetic life, Jerome gave himself up to a life of prayer, study, and writing, activities he would not easily interrupt to leave his monastery[104]—except to meet the demands of pastoral charity in leading souls to Christ through the study of the Scriptures.

St. Jerome's charismatic program of "sanctification through the Scriptures and the ascetic life" found a resonantly joyful reception in the community of nuns who gathered in the home of St. Marcella. Soon enough, these women would become a flock of spiritual daughters over whom he would lovingly expend himself for the rest of his life. In addition to Marcella herself, there was Albina, Marcella's mother; her sister, the saintly virgin Asella, whose praises Jerome sang while she was still alive;[105] the virgin Principia, Marcella's adopted daughter in the ascetic life; Marcellina, Felicity, and last, but certainly not least, the saintly widow Paula,[106] and her daughters, the young widow Blesilla and the virgin Eustochium.[107]

St. Paula, in particular, and her daughter St. Eustochium, would remain Jerome's faithful spiritual daughters to the end of their lives, and their virtuous souls would conquer Jerome's affection. Writing about Paula to Asella when about to leave Rome, he would enumerate the reasons why he loved Paula most especially:

> There was in Rome no other noblewoman who could so capture my mind, save she who always mourned and fasted, who, shabby and unkempt, was nearly rendered blind from many tears, and who would watch entire nights beseeching God for mercy till the sun would often find her still awake. She, whose songs of choice were Psalms, whose talk the Gospel, whose pleasure continence, and life itself a fast. No woman could bring me so much delight, save her whom never I beheld partake of food.[108]

When Jerome came to the Eternal City in the Fall of 382, his friends Epiphanius and Paulinus were hosted by Paula, who spared no expense in taking care of her illustrious guests. They expressed to her the hope of being able to repay her hospitality in their own lands, and she, desiring to take them up on their offer, promised to leave her homeland for the sake of Christ.[109] It seems, furthermore, that Epiphanius and Paulinus were the ones who introduced Jerome to Paula and the rest of Marcella's circle.[110]

As the young monk-priest was unaccustomed to speaking to nuns, especially women of noble rank, he initially displayed an understandable modesty in relating to them. Marcella, however, with conscientious wisdom, helped him ease out of his reticence by asking him questions about the Scriptures, since Jerome had a reputation for explaining them. Her questions challenged him, furthermore, and manifested the difficulties she encountered in reading them, so that she could confidently penetrate more deeply into the mysteries of the sacred text. Jerome addressed many of these questions in the fifteen or so letters he wrote to Marcella in this time, mainly in the year

384. They constitute a sort of course in Biblical exegesis for Marcella and the nuns she guided.

Deeply connected to his work in Scriptural education and exegesis was an attempt to form the women on the Aventine in the basic principles and practices of the monastic life. St. Jerome's strategy in this endeavor was twofold. First, he defined the hierarchy existing among the states of life of the women he encountered there based on the degree of their spousal commitment to Christ, the true Bridegroom of souls. Since consecrated virgins have renounced earthly marriage in order to be exclusively and definitively espoused to Christ, they occupy the highest place among the states of life of women. Consecrated widows, who upon the death of their first husbands have chosen Christ to be their second and definitive Bridegroom, occupy the second place.[111] Women who beget and rear children for Christ and the Kingdom of God in the context of a devout and chaste marriage occupy the third place. Jerome focused his efforts on speaking about the first order, that of virgins, perhaps because in doing so he would depict the spiritual ideal to which the other states should also tend.

The second element in Jerome's formative program was to propose for the emulation and veneration of all women (indeed, of all the faithful) she whose purity was such that she merited to be the Mother of the Lord: The Blessed Virgin Mary.[112] In the blessed fruit of Mary's womb, the Old Testament injunction to "be fruitful and multiply" found its happiest realization.[113] Moreover, the unblemished purity that characterized the Blessed Virgin before and after she bore Christ ushered in the grace of virginity, which previously enjoyed a limited expression in the lives of certain holy men (e.g. Elijah, Elisha, and Jeremiah), but was now lavished more abundantly upon the female sex. Accordingly, Mary brought an end to the Old Testament curse upon the unwed woman bereft of carnal progeny, and through her, the Son of God instituted on earth a family of celibate adherents whose singlehearted worship of Him mirrored the adoration given Him by the angels in heaven. Though the curse of death came through Eve, the blessing of life came through Mary.[114]

THE CONTROVERSY WITH HELVIDIUS

At this time in Rome, a treatise by a man named Helvidius was being circulated which denied Blessed Mary's virginity after the birth of Christ and, furthermore, the superiority of virginity over marriage. St. Jerome refrained from addressing the matter for much time but eventually conceded to the many requests of the faithful (among whom, we may assume, were the women on the Aventine) to refute the heretical propositions, which he did in a treatise defending the perpetual virginity of the Blessed Virgin Mary. The treatise is noteworthy since it is the first Mariological treatise written in Latin. St. Jerome succeeded so well in making his case that Our Lady's virginity was never again seriously questioned in Rome. To the end of guaranteeing Our Lady's virginal honor, he even argued that St. Joseph himself remained a virgin for the whole of his life. Indeed, how could anyone dare to assert that he touched the Mother of his Lord, the "temple of God and throne of the Holy Ghost," after having witnessed firsthand so many proofs of Christ's divinity?[115] Moreover, though some ecclesiastical writers claim that St. Joseph had wives apart from Mary so as to attribute to these the "brothers of the Lord" of which the Scripture speaks, the Scriptures themselves never say such a thing; to make such an inference, therefore, is rash, to say the least:

> But as we do not deny the things which have been set down in writing, so do we reject the things which have not been recorded. We believe that God was born from a Virgin because we read it. That Mary had marital relations after giving birth we do not believe because we do not read it. And neither do we say this because we reject marital intercourse, for virginity itself is a fruit of marital intercourse: but because we are not permitted to judge thoughtlessly concerning holy men. We can, indeed, in this rash evaluation of what is possible assert that Joseph had multiple wives because Abraham had many wives, as did Jacob; and that the "brothers of the Lord" are from these wives, as many contrive in thoughtlessness resulting not so much from piety as from audacity. You say that Mary did not remain a virgin: I, for my part, claim further that Joseph himself was a virgin for the sake of Mary, so that a virgin son should be born from a virginal marriage. If, indeed, adultery never befell the holy man, and it is not written that he had another wife; and he was the guardian, rather than the husband, of Mary, whom he was thought to have had as wife: it follows that he who merited to be called the father of the Lord remained a virgin along with Mary.[116]

There is another element that emerged in the treatise against Helvidius that would remain a mainstay of St. Jerome's polemical writings to the end of his life: satire. As a genre, satire was a literary form perfected by the classical Latin authors that Jerome knew so well, above all, Horace.[117] By means of it, Horace and the other great satirists of Roman antiquity sought to expose hypocrisy and unmask forms of moral corruption by means of parody and caricature, or ridicule an opponent's point of view to the extent of a *reductio ad absurdum*. As one scholar has observed,

> St. Jerome's great significance and importance as a Christian satirist lies not so much in his native ability and talents to use satire so brilliantly in all categories of his writings as in his ability to employ satire as an effective instrument in his dogmatic-polemical treatises in defending and defining so eloquently and so successfully the traditional views and doctrines of the Church . . . St. Jerome's program . . . embraced the entire body of views and doctrines of the Church. Consequently, his use and concept of satire was not determined by his own private views, but by the views of the Church. It was his honest and sincere belief that, when he attacked any individual and his heretical views, he was actually defending the Church. He had studied and absorbed the spirit and language and technique of the great classical satirists so thoroughly that satire became practically natural with him in any polemical work. Every form and type of satire in the classical tradition was used by him. It is difficult to distinguish an attack made by St. Jerome against an individual heretic from an attack on the whole heretic faction to which the individual belonged. Caution must be exercised at all times in attempting to judge or appraise the effectiveness or the appropriateness of any example of personal satire and invective employed by St. Jerome

> against individual heretics who are the main targets of his polemics in his doctrinal works for the simple reason that some of the important works and letters of these heretics which have given rise to the controversy are either entirely lost or are extant only as fragments . . . I believe that St. Jerome would not have been able to plead the cause of the Church so successfully in his dogmatic-polemical works . . . without his thorough knowledge and use of the classical satirical devices.[118]

Indeed, "to plead the cause of the Church" seems to have been a central part of St. Jerome's life and vocation. During his student days in Rome, one of his favorite pastimes was to attend court trials and listen to the fiery speeches that characterized the Roman litigation of his time.[119] Though this may not have been the best way for him to curb the strong irascible side of his nature, God eventually brought good from it nonetheless, and it may have initially inspired him to seek a career in the judiciary branch of Roman politics. The long sojourn he made in Triers after his Roman studies may have included some kind of apprenticeship in such a career. It was there, however, that he made the decision to consecrate his life to God as a monk. It is possible that an aspect of the call he then perceived was to employ his rhetorical skills, not in the defense of the emperor and the Roman state, and far less for the sake of personal gain, but in the service of the true King and Empire, i.e., Christ and His Militant Church upon earth. The way his life subsequently unfolded would certainly corroborate this hypothesis, for, in fact, he became one of God's most passionate jurists.

And it is in the treatise against Helvidius that we first encounter this dimension of the great doctor. Of the many salient examples of satire in this work, let us look at a few passages:

> O blind fury and senseless mind intent upon its own destruction! You say that at the Lord's cross His Mother was present, you say that she was entrusted to the disciple John on account of her solitary widowhood: as if, according to you, she didn't have four sons and countless daughters whose company she could have enjoyed?
>
> Most ignorant of men . . . you took your rabid fury to bring insult to the Virgin, in imitation of him concerning whom the fables speak, that, as he was unknown to the crowds, and could devise no decent deed by which he could win fame, set fire to Diana's temple. And as the sacrilege in no way brought about his purpose, it is reported he came forth into the midst of all and shouted out that he it was who sparked the conflagration. When the governors of Ephesus inquired why he chose to do this, he responded: So that by means of evil I could be well-known, since by means of good I could not do so. And this Greek history actually relates. But you set fire to the temple of the Lord's body, you have contaminated the sanctuary of the Holy Ghost, from which you fancy to have issued forth a four-fold team of brothers and a throng of sisters . . . .
>
> Please, tell me, who even knew you before you uttered forth this blasphemy? Who thought you worth a dime? You've gotten what you wanted, by your heinous deed you've gained renown. I myself, who write against you,

> though I live with you in the same City, don't know if you are white or black, as they say. I pass over the defects of your discourse, with which your whole book teems. I make no mention of your ridiculous first line, *O tempora! O mores!*[120]

Though the satirical approach we see employed here might strike modern readers as inappropriate, or even scandalous, it must be remembered that St. Jerome was writing at a time when the great Roman satirists of antiquity were read and valued, and their methods of argumentation were generally accepted. It should also be kept in mind that the bulk of the treatise against Helvidius sought to disprove, on the basis of Scripture, his heretical propositions, and although the satirical dimension is not lacking in those sections, it comes to a full blossom only at the end, in the passages we have quoted. The treatise against Helvidius, moreover, was written and well known in Rome when Pope St. Damasus was still alive, and he, Jerome informs us, found nothing reprehensible in the treatise.[121] Although, therefore, such manner of argumentation might be less understood, and therefore less appropriate today, it was, nevertheless, acceptable in St. Jerome's time. And he would soon make use of it again in a subsequent treatise on virginity which would thoroughly rattle his enemies, the history of which is now to be considered.

THE LETTER TO EUSTOCHIUM

In the late Spring of 384, St. Jerome sought to reinforce the points he articulated against Helvidius, consolidate and summarize the ascetical teaching he had imparted to his little flock on the Aventine, and denounce certain expressions of moral corruption that were threatening not only this group of nuns, but the very existence of monastic life in Rome. The occasion for doing so was the final taking of the veil of one of the women on the Aventine, Paula's third daughter, Julia Eustochium, in whose honor he wrote his celebrated treatise.[122]

Eustochium was just a child when her mother began frequenting Marcella's house to grow in the practice of the Faith. As such, she was half-raised by St. Marcella, who taught her not only the Faith, but also the basics of monastic prayer and discipline.[123] From these early days, therefore, Eustochium's heart was set on consecrating her life to Christ. But not all were happy about this prospect. Her uncle Hymetius, her father's pagan brother, was the most vocal of all, and sought ways to thwart his niece's purpose. At his bidding, therefore, his wife, Eustochium's aunt Prætextata, a high-born pagan herself, lured Eustochium away, and, spoiling her with worldly pastimes, fashionable hairstyles and makeup, and other trappings of self-indulgent pagan culture, persuaded her to momentarily set aside her monastic habit for worldly garb, so as to attract, it seems, a prominent and wealthy suitor. But Paula and Marcella's prayers won the day. After having seen all that the world had to offer, Eustochium chose Christ instead.[124] Nevertheless, she still needed guidance and protection given the unfavorable circumstances around her. As, therefore, it was St. Joseph's privileged duty to defend the Blessed Virgin Mary, so Jerome recognized his own duty, and that of every priest and bishop, to defend the honor and safety of Christ's cloistered brides and consecrated virgins. And he did so admirably in the letter *Audi Filia,* which he addressed to Eustochium, the City, and the world.

We can imagine that Eustochium, a graceful girl a few years shy of twenty, was flattered at receiving such a gift from one of the most prominent churchmen of her day. And although Jerome sought to strengthen her in her resolve by ascribing to her consecration to Christ the words St. Paul wrote in reference to the marriage of Christ and the Church—"This is that great Sacrament"—and by bestowing on her, as the Lord's bride, the noble title of *Domina* or *Dame*, he by no means sought to flatter her, for a flatterer is nothing but an enemy disguised in pleasant dress.[125] Rather, he would be brutally honest about the manifold foes which surrounded her, and her human frailty's urgent need of divine grace to overcome these adversaries. He thus identifies the principle vices against which she needed to wage war so as to enjoy her Bridegroom's embraces—vainglory, avarice, lust, and gluttony, which are to be countered with humble obedience to Christ, effective imitation of His poverty, fervent prayer, assiduous reading of Scripture, and tireless fasting. He places particular importance on the last of these, not because God is pleased with the rumbling of our empty stomachs, but because, Jerome is convinced, purity cannot be secured by any other means.

In addition to these internal enemies of the soul, Jerome meticulously exposes the human corruption by which Satan will try to tempt her from without, which is all the more pernicious because it cloaks itself with the vesture of religion. There are, to begin with, false virgins and widows, who take pleasure in the honor shown them on account of the chastity which they outwardly profess, and is visibly expressed in their religious garb, but who indulge in carnal pleasures no less than the licentious women of the world. Some of these find themselves with child out of wedlock, but are so attached to their honored status that they would rather abort their children in the womb than shamefully admit their fault. Such women, furthermore, are usually the ones who delight in elegant banquets and getting drunk in such contexts, but do not shrink from receiving Communion on the following day. Such women, and others who would ruin Eustochium in various ways, must be avoided at all costs.

Then there are false monks who wear long chains and who, against the Apostle's command, cultivate effeminately long hair. They love to visit noble women weighed down with sinful pasts. Such women are always learning, but never arriving at true knowledge, and these pseudo monks deceive them with their endless religious babble, sham fasts and feigned compunction.

Finally, there are men of Jerome's own priestly rank who aspired to the clerical state in order to enjoy the company of women under an honorable pretext. Such clerics are anxious over such things as being finely dressed, emitting the seductive fragrance of expensive cologne, and ensuring that their fancy leather shoes are made to fit just right. With curled hair and hands bedecked with shiny rings, they tiptoe lightly across a damp path, lest their feet get wet. Such men are to be reckoned wooers on the hunt, not priests. Jerome then, without saying any names, describes at length the leader of such men, so that by learning the arts of the master, his disciples may be unmasked as well. The ultimate intention of this old man's well-staged routine (indeed, he knows the town better than the post-man does) is to extort from rich women as many expensive fineries as possible.

One can well imagine the satirical caricature with which Jerome described these aspects of ecclesiastical corruption. It must have made Eustochium laugh, as it has many a reader since. To be sure, the letter *Audi Filia* can be scoured for sensational one-liners that provoke a good laugh, and this is probably, though unfortunately, the way it is often approached.

But the letter is far more than that. When read in the spirit in which it was composed—as a "word of salvation" from a spiritual father to his daughter in Christ—it can effectively lead one to the fear of God and genuine repentance, and must have brought Eustochium to tears. Even the satirical passages, when soberly considered, unmask appalling scandal in the Church, the full realization of which cannot but make one weep.

The letter climaxes to passages of remarkable beauty which exhort Eustochium—and us with her—to suffer all things for the Son of God, who for our salvation became man, was wrapped in swaddling clothes, and though securely holding the world in His tiny fist, endured to be contained within the narrow confines of the manger. He lived the majority of His life in humble subjection to His parents, and was at last beaten and crucified for us, and died while praying for His murderers. How shall we repay Him? Jerome replies with a whole series of biblical passages interspersed with memorable spiritual maxims: "I will take up the chalice of salvation, and call upon the name of the Lord. Precious in the eyes of the Lord is the death of his saints" (Ps. 115:5-6). This is the only worthy way we can repay Him, to shed our blood in gratitude for His, that those redeemed by Christ may willingly meet death for their Redeemer. Is it not better to sustain our battle for a little while, to carry our spear and bear our arms, and be exhausted under armor, and afterwards rejoice as conquerors, than serve eternally for having not withstood for one short hour? As Jacob's many years of toil seemed nothing due to his love for Rachel, so let us love Christ and seek out His embrace, and every trouble will seem easy. St. Paul says that "the sufferings of the present time are not worthy to be compared with the glory that is to be revealed in us" (Rom. 8:18); whenever, furthermore, the yoke you carry seems too much to bear, read his second letter to the Corinthians and you will see that in comparison, what you suffer is quite small. The Kingdom of Heaven suffers violence, and the violent take it by force (Matt. 11:12); unless, therefore, you strive with vehemence, you will not succeed in seizing it. As often as the vain ambitions of this age delight you, as often as you see something of glory in this world, travel with your mind to Paradise, and start already now to be that which you shall be then, and from your Bridegroom you shall hear: "Put me as a shelter in your heart; as a seal upon your arm" (Cant. 8:6), and fortified in soul and body, you shall cry to Him: "Many waters cannot quench love, nor rivers overwhelm it" (Cant. 8:7).

The Growing Antagonism Against Jerome

From early on, the letter *Audi filia* was widely circulated in the Western Church and even translated into Greek, as it proved to be a treatise of notable erudition, elegance, and spiritual depth.[126] But it was not these qualities that stood out for some people in the Roman ecclesiastical establishment, who, accurately, took it as an indictment on their moral corruption. Jerome, it will be remembered, had already aroused a good degree of unpopularity with his official revision of the Latin New Testament. His firm defense of the superiority of virginity and consecrated celibacy over marriage in the controversy with Helvidius and in the letter to Eustochium further embittered the people who already had a negative view of monasticism. Last, but not least, we can imagine that the high esteem Damasus showed toward him filled the priests of Rome with no little envy, a vice which, then as much as now, has always found a special home among the clergy. It was all too much for them to bear, and they started plotting how to rid themselves of this troublesome priest. So long as Damasus lived, Jerome was relatively safe. But as the year started to decline, so did Damasus's health. On December 11, 384, Pope St. Damasus died in the odor of sanctity, admirably bringing his illustrious eighteen-year pontificate to a close.

Soon after Damasus's death, Pope Siricius was chosen as his successor. The new pope was a meek and simple man, but wholly uninterested in the cultural and scholarly concerns that preoccupied Damasus. As such, it would have been difficult for him to appreciate the Scriptural and theological contributions made by St. Jerome. And, although he personally did not try to get of rid of the erudite monk, neither was he going to protect him from the growing animosity of those who sought to oust him from the Roman ecclesiastical scene. They tried to do so, it seems, by accusing him of coercing women to live the monastic life, and, moreover, by alleging that he had committed the same offense which he had so forcefully censured in other priests, i.e., of amorously seducing a Roman matron—in this case Paula—in order to rob her of her money.

This unfortunate scheme of lies and half-truths begins to come into focus for us in Jerome's account of the funeral of Paula's eldest daughter, Blesilla. In the letter *Audi filia,* Jerome had alluded to Blesilla as an example of the precariousness of married life in the world, since her husband had died just seven months after they were married, leaving her a widow in the prime of her youth.[127] As a married woman, and even for a time after her husband's premature death, she was somewhat far from the Faith and given over to worldly pastimes, which were not hard to come by for a young woman of her wealth and rank. Though the pious examples of her mother and younger sister were insufficient to rouse her from these vanities, God succeeded in bringing about her remarkable conversion through a violent fever that consumed her for an entire month, and in the course of which she obtained, like King Hezekiah of old, a *spatium veræ penitentiæ*, i.e., an interval of sincere repentance by means of which she could convert her heart to the Lord.[128]

Upon recovering from her illness, she hastened to the spiritual transformation to which she felt called. She took St. Jerome as her spiritual father, who nurtured her in the love of God and helped bring to maturity her budding contempt for the world by reading and explaining to her the book of Ecclesiastes (or *Coelet*, as it is known in Hebrew).[129] As she was talented in languages, and spoke Greek as fluently as her native Latin, she arrived at an admirable competency in Hebrew in just a few days, surpassing Origen and even Jerome himself in their swiftness to learn, and started vying with her mother in memorizing and singing the Psalms in their original language. But, more importantly, the level of sanctity she reached equally as quickly manifested itself in the deep humility that permeated her every word and gesture.

But her sickness, which had been dormant for three months, soon returned. Notwithstanding her faltering steps, her pale and trembling countenance, and scarce ability to hold her head upright, she always had the Prophets or the Gospels in hand. When even this was not possible, she turned to those near her and implored them with tearful groans "to pray to the Lord Jesus to forgive me because I was not able to accomplish that which I desired."[130] Soon thereafter she died in sure repentance and deep love for God, and compressed plentiful seasons of virtue into the span of a short life.[131]

We can imagine how distressed her loved ones were at her sudden departure from this life. Jerome, Marcella, Eustochium, and Paula, felt as if they had lost a great treasure. Everyone was overcome with grief, but nobody more than poor Paula, who had much difficulty accepting the premature death of her eldest daughter. As she was a deeply sensitive woman, and easily given over to tears, she wept for Blesilla even more than she did for her late husband, at whose passing, Jerome informs us, her uncontainable tears seemed to indicate her own proximate death.[132] Indeed, midway through the funeral procession, crippled by her woeful lamentations, Paula had to remove herself from the company of the others in order to give way to her grief.

The incident was not lost on the antagonists of the monastic life and enemies of St. Jerome, who began to gossip among themselves and assert that Paula was lamenting the fact that her daughter was "killed by excessive fasting" and that she had never contracted a second marriage, from which Paula could have had grandchildren. "How long until that detestable order of monks is expelled from the City, assailed with stones, and thrown headlong into the Tiber?" they began to exclaim. "They have beguiled a pitiable noble woman who never wanted to be a nun, as is evident from the fact that she weeps for her dead daughter more than any pagan woman ever wept for her dead children."

Paula's extreme grief was, consequently, a scandal. For a Christian, it was disproportionate and indicative of a lack of faith in God and the Resurrection of Christ. For days after the funeral, she refused to take food and continued to indulge in bitter tears. Jerome had to intervene, and wrote a notable letter to Paula (*Letter 39* to Paula, *Quis dabit*) that sought not only to console her, but also to rebuke her—such was his duty as her spiritual father—for her injurious fasting and excessive tears, which were loathsome because they manifested a culpable lack of faith and a spirit of rebellion to the designs of God's providence. The letter, therefore, did not lack the stern "bite of truth,"[133] though it also abounded in the honey of consolation, and would mark the first of many such epitaphs Jerome would write in order to proclaim the virtues of a departed saint and to console surviving loved ones in their grief.

Though it must have been a tough read for the sorrowful Paula, the letter had a salutary effect on her. With time she was able to move beyond the pain of Blesilla's death, and the solid arguments Jerome had used to prompt her on to a greater faith in and more complete surrender to God not only re-kindled, but also greatly fueled her burning desire to forsake homeland and loved ones in order to follow Christ. Mindful of the invitations the bishops Paulinus and Epiphanius had extended to her a few years previously, she began the practical arrangements to leave Rome for good and sail eastward.

The momentary lapse of her uncontrolled grief, however, had left an unsightly blemish on both the monastic community as well as St. Jerome's reputation. Regardless of the truth concerning Blesilla's conversion and death, the mob that was inimical to him began to brand him as a merciless ascetic who coerced women to become nuns, then killed them through excessive fasting. The fact that Paula was now preparing to leave everything in order to become a nun in the Holy Land, presumably with Jerome's blessing, gave them grounds to hurl their most pernicious accusation yet. Some unnamed man denounced Jerome to the public authorities as a swindler who was seducing Paula. Though the liar subsequently recanted the accusation and acknowledged Jerome's innocence, the harm done to Jerome's reputation was irreparable, and he had to leave the City, initially taking refuge in the neighboring countryside before leaving Italy altogether later that summer.[134]

FAREWELL, ETERNAL CITY

Although we know Jerome left Italy in August of AD 385, it is not clear when Paula and Eustochium did. Nevertheless, it seems reasonable to assume they did so shortly after Jerome set sail,[135] and that both parties eventually reunited at some established point on the journey. However, let us consider Paula's dramatic departure first.

Returning to the epic letter Jerome wrote to Heliodorus while he was still in the deserts of Chalcis[136] would be helpful as it seems to have influenced Paula's decision to forsake her family, and the vivid images of that letter accord well with the description of Paula's departure from Rome. It will be recalled that Jerome wrote this letter in order to persuade Heliodorus to forsake his homeland and loved ones so that he could become a monk. Accordingly, he wrote:

> Though your infant nephew should dangle from your neck, though your mother should, with tousled hair and garments rent, display the breasts with which she fed you, though your father sprawl himself over the

> threshold, trampling over him proceed, with tearless eyes make speed unto the standard of the Cross. OF PIETY there is no other sort, than in this matter to be cruel.[137]

This dramatic scene, which Jerome described to Heliodorus as a *hypothetical* situation he might face in forsaking his loved ones, became *actual* in the life of Paula. The reality Paula lived through, was, however, far more dramatic than the imaginary situation envisaged by Jerome; for while there it concerned a young man forsaking his mother and father, in Paula's case it was the *mother* forsaking her children, one of whom, Toxotius, was still a little boy!

> Mindful not of home, nor children, nor household, nor possessions, nor any other thing belonging to this world, alone (if this can be said) and unaccompanied, she keenly longed to journey to the desert colonized by many an Anthony and Paul. At last, with winter past, and with the sea accessible and open, as the bishops (i.e., Paulinus and Epiphanius) sailed back to their churches, she also put to sea—although by means of solemn promise and desire. Why should I furthermore delay? She went down to the port with brother, in-laws, relatives, and what is more, with her own children following behind her, desiring to overcome that gentlest of mothers through compassion. The sailing canvas was by now unfurled, and by the rowing of the oars the ship was borne aloft. At the shore the small Toxotius stretched forth beseeching hands. Ruffina, now of marriageable age, and as she hoped to be wed soon, implored with silent sobs. And

> yet, that woman turned her tearless eyes to heaven, by means of piety towards God defeating piety towards her very children. She was unmindful of her status as a mother to verify she was the handmaid of the Lord. Her bowels turned within her, and with the pain she fought as if she were disjointed from her very members: in this, though, more admirable still was that she conquered love so great. Amidst the hands of enemies and harsh constraints of bondage, nothing is more brutal than for parents to be split up from their children. This, against the laws of nature, a faith robust endured, nay, more, a soul rejoicing sought: and deeming slight love for her children through a greater love for God, she found rest in Eustochium alone, who with her shared one common aim and journey. And as the ship began to plough across the sea, and all those being borne away with her fixed eager gazes at the shore, she firmly turned her eyes away, so that she would not see those whom she could not see without distress. I readily declare, that thus no woman ever loved her children, on whom she lavished all before departing, disinheriting herself on earth, in order to acquire an inheritance in heaven.[138]

Few passages in the hagiographical literature, if any, could rival this magnificent description of St. Paula's parting from her family, impressive as it is for both the astonishing scene it relates, as well as the exquisitely poetic language used to recount it. The episode described cannot help but unsettle most people, for it makes shockingly clear the absolute and divine sovereignty of Jesus Christ in the life of a believer, and how the claims of His love override those of every other love—be it that of child, parent, or spouse. It disquiets us believers because it forces us to consider the loves we tend to put above the love of Christ in practice, and, therefore, challenges us to put our loves in order—perhaps at the cost of what is dearest to us. In ways similar to Paula's heartrending separation from her family, the perennial option of monks and nuns to consecrate themselves entirely to Christ makes tangible, in every age, those unsettling words of Christ: "Do not think that I came to send peace upon earth: I came not to send peace, but the sword. For I came to set a man at variance against his father, and the daughter against her mother, and the daughter-in-law against her mother-in-law. And a man's enemies shall be they of his own household. He that loveth father or mother more than me is not worthy of me: and he that loveth son or daughter more than me is not worthy of me" (Matt. 10:34-37). A clear proof of St. Paula's heroic and magnanimous virtue is that she loved her children not only deeply, but even vehemently, and yet, in the words of St. Jerome, "more admirable still was that she conquered love so great *(in eo cunctis admirabilior, quod magnam vinceret caritatem)*" for the sake of a greater love, that of Jesus Christ.

Jerome's Departure

A few days prior to Paula and Eustochium's momentous departure, Jerome himself sailed to the Holy Land from the port of Rome accompanied by Fr. Vincent, Eusebius of Cremona, his younger brother Paulinian, and other monks, with a throng of Catholic faithful trailing behind him to say goodbye.[139]

As soon as he had a moment of calm, he wrote his last letter from Italy. It was a note of gratitude to someone he highly esteemed, Marcella's sister, the virgin recluse Asella. When Jerome first befriended Marcella and her circle, she told him about the singular life of this holy woman, a genuine desert mother in the midst of the hustle and bustle of Rome. Like Jeremiah and John the Baptist, from the womb she, too, was consecrated to a holy way of life, and from the age of twelve she resolutely devoted herself to seeking God in the narrow confines of her cell, finding there a paradise of peace in prayer. Jerome marveled at her impressive fasting and other ascetical feats, and especially her fervent prayer, austere joy, and eloquent silence. Her goodness elicited the spontaneous praise of the virtuous and rendered her impervious to the detraction of the wicked. Not only widows and virgins but even married women looked up to her as a pattern to imitate, and the wicked feared her, while priests revered her.[140]

As she was a recluse, and, therefore, somewhat removed from the intense drama Jerome had recently lived through, he was able to find comfort in her, and, consequently, turned to her as to a spiritual mother. To Marcella and the other women of the Aventine he had to be the knowledgeable teacher who had the answers to their questions about the Scriptures; to Paula and Eustochium he had to be the confident spiritual father, always ready to indicate the next step; to Asella, however, he could be a son, and trustfully confide to her maternal prayers his insecurities and sorrows, his faults and insufficiencies, and his need for God's love in the midst of the tempests of his life.

Asella had communicated that love to him somehow, perhaps through a letter or some keepsake she sent him. Although we do not know how exactly, we do know that the gesture of kindness she extended to Jerome meant the world to him. We can gather as much from the opening lines of the memorable letter he wrote to her.

> I'd be a fool to think that I could adequately thank you. God is able to repay your holy soul on my behalf that which it merits. Indeed, I am unworthy, and could never have imagined, nor yet hoped, that you would lavish on me such affection in the Lord. And though some may consider me a scoundrel, and submerged beneath a torrent of disgraces—and, though, these even for my sins be slight: in this, however, you do well: that from your heart you reckon noble even the despicable.[141]

In the rest of the letter, Jerome tries to make sense of the painful situation in which he finds himself and, consequently, summarizes for Asella the unfortunate circumstances that led to his departure. It reads like an imaginary court trial in which he defends himself against, and even directly addresses, his enemies. He states the opinion many people have of him based on the accusations made against him, i.e., that he is "shameful, duplicitous, and perilous, a liar who beguiles others by demonic arts."[142] Then, after adamantly defending his innocence *vis-à-vis* the accusations brought against him, he points out what must have motivated his detractors to defame him: pure and simple envy. It stirred envy among the "who's who" of Rome that he should have had such admiration for the noble woman Paula and her virtues. It disquieted their conscience that she and her daughter Eustochium, under Jerome's influence, should have forsaken all things to follow Christ. The excellence of their lives was an affront to their pride, for it manifested their mediocrity. Rather than admit the higher nobility of their lives, they preferred to tarnish their reputation by means of calumny. And since it was Jerome, the recognized spokesman for the monastic cause, who encouraged them upon this course, he became the ultimate target of their calumnies.

In the final lines of the letter, Jerome calls himself a fool for having deserted the sacred regions of the East, made holy by Christ and His Apostles, and expresses his intention to return there now definitively. Though his sojourn in Rome has brought him much suffering, he rejoices in the fact that such trials inevitably befall the soldier who fights under the standard of the Cross, thereby confirming his identity as a *miles crucis*. After addressing words of respectful affection to Asella, and sending greetings to his dear ones in Rome, he asks her to protect his imminent voyage by her prayers.

> With tears and sorrow, now that I have boarded ship, I've quickly written down these things, my Dame, Asella, and I thank my God that I am worthy to be one whom this world hates. Pray, though, that from this Babylon unto Jerusalem I may return, lest Nebuchadnezzar govern me, but, rather, Jesus, the son of Josedec. Let Ezras come, whose name means *helper*, and lead me once again into my homeland. I am a fool, because I wished to sing the Lord's canticle in a foreign land, and having left behind Mount Sinai, went beseeching Egypt for assistance (Jer. 42). I forgot the Gospel, that whoever leaves Jerusalem at once falls in with robbers, and is stripped, wounded and slain. And though even the Priest and Deacon look down with disdain, that Samaritan is merciful (Lk. 10), who, when they told him: *You're*

a Samaritan and have a demon (Jn. 8), rejecting the part about the demon, did not object to being a Samaritan, for he whom we call *guardian*, the Hebrews call *Samaritan*. Some scandalmongers call me an enchanter; I, a servant of the Lord, accept it as a title of fidelity. The Jews, as well, call my Lord a magician. The Apostle, too, was labeled a seducer. No temptation, save for a human one, has taken hold of me (1 Cor. 10). What trifle of distress have I, who soldier for the Cross, endured? They charged me with the infamy of a false crime: I know, however, that through good and bad repute one can attain unto the realms of heaven.

Greet Paula and Eustochium, who, whether the world wishes it or not, are mine in Christ. Greet your mother Albina, and your sister Marcella, and also Marcellina, and devout Felicity, and tell them: We shall likewise stand before the judgment seat of Christ, there shall come to light the mindset with which each of us has lived. Remember me, O eminent exemplar of virginity and purity; and by your prayers mitigate the billows of the sea.[143]

Chapter 7

Jerome's Second Period in the East

Et tu, Bethlehem

Jerome's first stop after setting sail was Rhegium, modern-day Reggio, in Calabria, on the Straits of Messina, where he paused to contemplate the setting of some of the most memorable scenes from Homer's epic poem *The Odyssey*. The locals there warned him to avoid the southern part of the Mediterranean, off the coast of Alexandria, but, rather, to stay closer to the coast of Greece in order to arrive more safely at Cyprus. There he enjoyed the hospitality of his friend, St. Epiphanius. From Cyprus, he and his fellow monks made their way to Antioch, where they stayed some time with his friend and bishop, Paulinus.[144]

Paula and Eustochium followed close behind Jerome on the same nautical path, except for a stop *en route* to Rhegium at the island of Pontia, where they venerated the places made holy by the martyr St. Flavia Domitilla, who was exiled there under the emperor Domitian. After Rhegium, they, too, stayed as guests of St. Epiphanius on Cyprus, touring the monasteries of the island so as to benefit from their life of prayer and leave behind care packages for the monks.[145] From Cyprus they traveled to Antioch via the port city of Seleucia. It was probably in Antioch that they met up with Jerome and his party, and in the middle of a very cold winter, began their journey south toward Jerusalem and Bethlehem, stopping at every place made holy by the events of sacred history.

Jerome tells us this was his first time seeing the holy places in and around Jerusalem. But rather than tell us his impressions on that memorable journey, he describes at length the prayerful devotion Paula displayed at each place. Indeed, she showed such loving diligence in venerating every holy place and object, that it seemed she would have stayed fixed in each place, had there not been yet other sights to see.[146] Particularly striking is the devotion she displayed toward Bethlehem and the sacred cave of Christ's Nativity, which we shall describe after relating the whole of their pilgrimage.

From Bethlehem, Jerome and Paula's company went to Egypt and toured the deserts inhabited by the Desert Fathers. Here, too, Paula's effusive devotion manifested itself, venerating each monk as if he were Christ, and considered every gift she made to them as if made to Christ Himself. Indeed, her love for the monastic life was so great that she would have gladly embraced the desert as her own home, had not her desire to dwell amidst Christ's holy places been greater.[147] Although Jerome shared her enthusiasm, he later admitted to have observed a few "snakes" hiding amidst the choirs of saints in the desert, by whom he probably meant those of heretical leanings.

Jerome and Paula's company made one last stop in Alexandria before returning to Palestine. Paula, in particular, wanted to go there, and Jerome admits to having gone there at her bidding.[148] Nevertheless, he, too, wished to visit the Egyptian metropolis, above all to meet and to listen to the renowned teacher Didymus the Blind.[149] Truly, this man was a living wonder of the ancient world, for Jerome tells us that though he was deprived of his eyes from a young age, and consequently illiterate, he nevertheless stunned the world by achieving a mastery not only in logic but also in geometry, the science which most requires the gift of sight. He dictated so many dogmatic treatises and commentaries on Scripture (not a few at Jerome's bidding) that he alone could recount the full list of them.[150] Writing some fifteen years later, Jerome recalls gratefully the time he spent with Didymus, who taught him much he did not know, and reinforced that which he did know in such a way that he never forgot it.[151] Indeed, though he was blind, Jerome calls Didymus "his seer"[152] on account of his uncanny ability to peer into the deepest mysteries, a spiritual vision far superior to physical sight. Jerome recounts a remarkable episode in which St. Anthony the Great helped Didymus to understand the greatness of the gift he had received. When, at the request of St. Athanasius, St. Anthony came to Alexandria in order to refute the Arian heretics, Didymus sought out the renowned monk in order to speak about the Scriptures and the spiritual life with him. After having expressed admiration for his exceptional genius and spiritual perception, St. Anthony probed Didymus a bit, saying, "You're not sad because you lack the eyes of the flesh, are you?" After hesitating somewhat due to shame, Didymus humbly confessed that he was. St. Anthony responded to him in words that must have humbled him even as they exalted him, saying, "I marvel at the fact that a man as prudent as you are is sorrowful because he lacks something which even ants, mosquitoes and flies have, and does not, rather, rejoice in the possession of that which only saints and Apostles have merited to enjoy."[153] It was this, Didymus's spiritual vision, which Jerome sought in Alexandria, and after having greatly benefited from it, he and his company returned to the Holy Land.

Of all the places they had seen in and around Jerusalem, it was Bethlehem that most captured the hearts of Paula and Jerome; consequently, it was there they chose to settle and live their monastic life. As they were of one accord on this point, we can gather Jerome's own sentiments for the place from his lovely description of Paula's devotion to Bethlehem. After concluding their trip to Jerusalem with a visit to Mt. Sion, Jerome says that:

> Then according to her scanty means, as she gave her money to the poor her fellow servants, she made her way to Bethlehem . . . and walking in the Savior's cave, after she beheld the Virgin's hostel, and the stable in which *the ox knew his owner and the ass his master's crib* (Is. 1:3) . . . I heard her solemnly declare that with the eyes of faith she saw the infant wrapped in swaddling clothes, the Lord crying in the manger, the Magi adoring Him, the star shining above, the Virgin Mother, their guardian solicitous for them, the shepherds coming in the night to see the Word which had been made (Luc. 2:16); and thus, affirm already the beginning of John's Gospel: *In the beginning was the Word, and the Word was made flesh (Jn. 1)*; then the slaughtered children, Herod plotting cruelty, Joseph and Mary fleeing into Egypt: and mingling joy with tears, would say: Hail *Bethlehem, house of bread,* in which was born that Bread who from the heavens condescended. Hail *Ephrata,* plentiful and

> lavish kingdom, rich in choicest fruits, whose fruitfulness is God Himself. Once concerning you Micah foretold: *And Thou, BETHLEHEM Ephrata, art a little one among the thousands of Juda; out of thee shall he come forth unto me that is to be the ruler in Israel: and his going forth is from the beginning, from the days of eternity. (Mic. 5:2-3).* In you, indeed, was born the Prince, who prior to the day star was begotten (Ps. 109): He, whose birth is from the Father and transcends all ages... And is it possible that I, a wretched sinner, have been found worthy to kiss that manger wherein the Newborn Lord first cried? To pray, moreover, in the cave in which the childbearing Virgin brought forth the Infant Lord? Here shall be my resting place, for it is my Lord's fatherland. Here shall I dwell, for it the Savior chose ... Close to it Jacob fed his flocks, and shepherds keeping watch at night deserved to hear: *Gloria in excelsis Deo et in terra pax hominibus bonæ voluntatis (Lk. 2:14).* And as they kept their sheep, they came upon the Lamb of God in pure and spotless fleece, which rained upon the arid earth in a celestial dewfall (Jd. 6:37).[154]

In this admirable passage we perceive the ardent love which the Latin Church has always cherished for the mystery of the Incarnation; indeed, the passage probably did much to foster that love. Long before St. Francis and St. Cajetan recreated their scenes of the Nativity, before the artistic masterpieces of the West depicting Christ's Nativity, before the magnificent Gregorian hymn "A solis ortus" and a host of other carols were composed, before the Roman Liturgy perfected its epic, poetic Christmas cycle, St. Paula and St. Jerome devoted their lives to

Christ's Nativity by living in Bethlehem, so as to always contemplate its mysteries. They found such peace in this humble place that Paula and Eustochium emphasized it, above all, when writing to Marcella, their beloved teacher and spiritual mother, inviting, indeed, begging her to leave Rome, and join them in Bethlehem:

> And truly when it comes to Christ's small village, and Mary's hostel, what word, what utterance could adequately set forth the Savior's cave? And that manger crib, in which the blessed Infant first gave forth his sobs, is honored more by silence than unsteady words . . . Behold in this small burrow of the earth, the Maker of heaven was born; here He was wrapped in swaddling clothes, here He was seen by shepherds, here He was shown by a star, here He was adored by the Magi.[155]

Jerome summarized all these sentiments by consistently referring to Bethlehem as more august than Rome itself, indeed, as the most majestic place on earth.[156]

JEROME IN BETHLEHEM

After his pilgrimage touring the sites in Palestine and Egypt, Jerome's travels became considerably less distant and less frequent. He had left his country and loved ones so that, like Abraham, he could voluntarily embrace exile, as was common for monks in those days. The purpose, furthermore, of his recent travels was to acquire a deeper understanding of both the monastic life as well as of the sacred page by seeing the places where monasticism was born and the events of salvation history took place. But he had now seen enough of the world, and understood more deeply that God was present everywhere, be it Gaul or Palestine; that the true homeland of every Christian was the heavenly Jerusalem above; and that we best prepare ourselves to take hold of that heavenly citizenship by becoming God's dwelling place here below. As he wrote in a letter to St. Paulinus of Nola:

> It is not praiseworthy simply to have been in Jerusalem, but to have lived well in Jerusalem. That city is to be sought, that city is to be praised which is made joyful by the flowing of the river (Ps. 45:4; Lk. 11): which is placed on top of the mountain so that it cannot be concealed: which the Apostle calls the mother of the saints, and in which he rejoices to have citizenship with the souls of the just.
>
> But in saying this I do not rebuke myself of inconstancy, nor condemn that which I do: as if it had been futile that I abandoned family and homeland in imitation of Abraham: but, rather, I dare not enclose the omnipotence of God in narrow boundaries, nor restrict Him whom the heavens cannot contain in a tiny corner of the earth. Every believer will be assessed by the merit of his faith, not by the diversity of his dwelling. What is more, the true worshippers adore the Father neither in Jerusalem nor on Mt. Garizim: for God is spirit, and His worshippers must worship in spirit and in truth. "But the Spirit breathes where He wills. The Lord's is the earth and the fullness thereof" (Jn. 3:8; Ps. 23:1) . . . Consequently, the places of both the Cross and the Resurrection avail those who daily bear their cross, and daily rise with Christ, those who show themselves to be

> His worthy dwelling places. For the rest, let those who say, *it is the Temple of the Lord, the Temple of the Lord* (Jer. 7), hear the Apostle say: *You are the Lord's temple, and the Holy Spirit dwells within you (2 Cor. 6:16).* And the gates of heaven are equally open to both Jerusalem and Brittany, for *The Kingdom of God is within you.*[157]

Indeed, Jerome was now to settle down and concentrate on the work to which God had called him, which was first and foremost the spiritual work of conversion and growth in humility.[158] To this end, he wanted the solitude and peace he had once tasted as a young hermit in the deserts of Chalcis. He wanted to be hidden in his cell to expect the day of judgment, weep for his sins, and *be* a genuine Christian, rather than merely seem one.[159]

Moreover, he also felt the demand of Christian charity to serve God and neighbor in concrete ways. He and his brother monks would thus instruct others in the faith, often preparing them to receive the sacraments.[160] They would also receive and provide for all the guests that would come to them—except for heretics, of course.[161] Indeed, one of the ways his charity most expressed itself was in defending the truths of the Catholic faith, which often entailed fighting heresies both close to home and abroad. St. Jerome's activity as a staunch opponent of heresy is particularly praised by Sulpicius Severus, his contemporary as well as biographer of St. Martin of Tours, who includes a section on St. Jerome and his manner of life in Bethlehem in his work the *Dialogues.*[162]

But the immensely demanding and greatly toilsome work that most absorbed St. Jerome in Bethlehem, and consequently, took the place of his manual labor, was that of translating and explaining the Scriptures for the Church of both present and future.[163] From the year 386, by when St. Jerome had fully established himself in Bethlehem, until 392, the year in which he published his book *De Viris Illustribus,* the list of his written works is astonishing. It comprises no less than ten Biblical Commentaries (on Galatians, Ephesians, Titus, Philemon, Ecclesiastes, Micah, Sophonia, Nahum, Habacuc, and Haggai), three Biblical treatises (Questions on Genesis, Concerning places, on Hebrew Names), the two *Lives* of the monk Malchus and of St. Hilarion, a staggering number of translations from Greek and Hebrew (Didymus's *De Spiritu Sancto,* thirty-nine homilies of Origen on Luke, his revision of the New Testament and much of his translation of the Old Testament), seven treatises on the Psalms, a dogmatic treatise comprising two books against Jovinian and an apology of the same treatise, and, finally, his book *De Viris Illustribus.* In order for him to have accomplished such a feat in these six years, we must conclude that he was not only endowed with a superhuman industriousness, but also that he did little else besides study and write. Sulpicius Severus corroborates this conclusion, for he relates of St. Jerome that he was "always absorbed in reading, entirely amidst books, resting neither by day nor by night, but always reading or writing something." [164]

Sulpicius also informs us that Jerome governed the church (ecclesiam) of Bethlehem, by which we presume he meant the community of monks who settled with him, and not the parish church, which, as Sulpicius also notes, belonged to the Bishop of Jerusalem, and was, presumably, entrusted to the pastoral care of his priests.[165] Indeed, although it is difficult, though possible, to reconcile Jerome's enormous written output in these years with the duties of a monastic superior, to think that he was additionally absorbed in the numerous priestly duties incumbent on the pastor of a rural parish—one, moreover, continually bustling with pilgrims—seems unthinkable. The "church," therefore, which St. Jerome governed, was in all likelihood the community of monks who settled with him. As to the manner of life of this community, there is no reason to think that it differed substantially from the observance they had in Rome with regard to communal prayer and fasting practices, and Jerome informs us that he continued to impart to them the fruits of his learning in homilies and spiritual conferences on Scripture.[166]

There is one final observation Sulpicius makes of St. Jerome that now must be explored. He relates how at the time, Alexandria and the Egyptian desert were being torn apart by the strife of Origenism, a system of theology and spirituality based on certain tenets of the Alexandrian master, Origen. As we have seen, Jerome highly venerated Origen since his days as a student in Antioch and Constantinople. "But," Sulpicius remarks, "this disquieted me considerably: that Jerome, a man in all things Catholic and highly expert in the sacred law, though formerly reckoned to be a follower of Origen, now condemns especially Origen, and all his writings."[167] It is to the Origenist controversy, and Jerome's involvement in it, that we must now turn.

ADVERSUS ORIGENEM

In addition to his deep devotion to the Infant Christ and His Virgin Mother, St. Jerome probably had other reasons for deciding to settle in Bethlehem. One of these was to be closer to the library of Cæsarea in Palestine, where an exemplar of

Origen's famous *Hexapla* was kept. The *Hexapla* was one of Origen's finest accomplishments, for in it he laid out, in six adjacent columns, six versions of the Hebrew Scriptures: the original in Hebrew, a Greek transliteration of the Hebrew, the Septuagint, and three other Greek translations made by Aquila, Theodotius, and Symmachus. Jerome copied out much, if not the whole of this work, for his own continuous reference in explaining the Old Testament.

Another likely reason he settled in Bethlehem was to be near his friends, one of whom was St. Epiphanius. Epiphanius, himself once a monk in the deserts of Egypt, continued to exert a formative influence over the monks of Egypt and Palestine, and as a bishop was one of the most esteemed prelates of the time. As we have seen, he had been an important friend and mentor to Jerome since the time of Jerome's priestly ordination in Antioch some fifteen years earlier, and was instrumental in helping Jerome forge some of his most important relationships during his second sojourn in Rome (i.e., Pope Damasus and the women on the Aventine). As Epiphanius was a bishop in nearby Cyprus and came to Palestine frequently to visit his monastery in Eleutheropolis, Jerome would have had frequent opportunities to see and consult him.

The other friend whose presence in Palestine probably influenced Jerome's decision to settle there was Rufinus, who for years had been living as a monk on the Mount of Olives in Jerusalem. Jerome's friendship with Rufinus dated back to at least his first monastic experience in Aquileia, if not earlier. Shortly after the end of that experience Jerome wrote a letter to Rufinus during his sojourn in Antioch, before settling in the deserts of Chalcis (*Letter 3, Plus Deum*). It is a letter written in the "languor of youth"—to borrow an expression of

Evelyn Waugh—a time in which generous, and even effusive, expressions of affection come naturally to friends. In addition to catching his old friend up on the ups and downs of his travels since they last saw each other, Jerome conveyed many such expressions of ardent affection in this letter. Beyond a probable complementarity of natural temperament, such affection probably flourished in these two men due to the literary and rhetorical formation they had received, which produced in them a common love for study and literary eloquence. Eventually deepened by a common love for the Christian faith and the monastic life, such a friendship seemed to all to be a genuine treasure. But there was one additional common interest that would eventually make them bitter enemies, although it initially drew them closer together.

This common interest was their love for Origen. As we have seen, since his student days in Constantinople, and perhaps even earlier, Jerome nurtured a genuine veneration for the great linguist, philosopher, and theologian. It is likely that he transferred the admiration he had for Cicero and other pagan authors to Origen, finding in his writings the literary beauty he once treasured in theirs. He marveled at Origen's zeal for studying the Scriptures and at his prodigious literary output expounding them. Jerome translated many of Origen's works, adopted his exegetical methods and patterned his life on his example of study coupled with asceticism. During his second sojourn in Rome, Jerome translated two of Origen's homilies on the Canticle of Canticles for Pope Damasus and wrote notable letters extolling the Alexandrian genius to the consecrated women on the Aventine.[168] Once established in Bethlehem, he translated Origen's homilies on the Gospel of Luke and relied much on Origen's exegesis in making his own commentaries on the Pauline epistles. When he published his catalogue of Ecclesiastical writers, *De Viris Illustribus*, in 392, he included a substantial and enthusiastic entry on Origen. Up to this point, therefore, Jerome had a positive stance toward Origen.

But toward the end of this period we start to observe some caution in Jerome's approach to Origen, above all in his Commentary on Ephesians. This Pauline Epistle, with its grand cosmic themes, had furnished Origen with ample opportunity for advancing some of his most peculiar teachings, such as the preexistence of souls and their consequent "falling" into bodies as a punishment for some primordial sin; an indefinitely mutable nature of rational creatures which allowed for angels to suffer a reprehensible "demotion" and thus become either men or demons, and, alternatively, the possibility of demons returning to their former position as good angels; a negative view of the human body which likens it to a punishing shackle or chain; and, finally, the belief that in the end there will be a complete rehabilitation of the souls of damned angels and men, known as the *apocatastasis*.[169]

Confronted with teachings so manifestly contrary to Christian revelation, Jerome simply could not overlook them and act as if Origen never taught such things, or, even worse, compromise his own faith and adapt himself to the errors of Origen. But, as Origen still enjoyed a positive reputation in the Christian world and Jerome himself still cherished a deep respect for him and continued to benefit from the many good things he found in his writings, he did not want to openly denounce him as a heretic either. He thus chose a moderate approach and set forth the heterodox teachings of Origen (without attributing them explicitly to him) alongside orthodox interpretations, favoring the latter in the hopes of inducing the judicious reader to discard the former. This approach had the benefit of allowing Jerome to continue in his positive view toward Origen without embracing his errors. But its weakness was a certain ambiguity regarding these teachings that might give a non-judicious reader, or one blindly attached to Origen, the impression that Jerome himself espoused those unorthodox beliefs.

As Jerome began to see these errors more clearly in his study of Origen, he probably also felt a push from Epiphanius to openly distance himself from these and other problematic teachings of Origen. As early as the mid-370s, Epiphanius had written extensively on the various heresies and heresiarchs that had plagued the Church up to that time, and devoted considerable attention to the heresies of Origen.[170] As Epiphanius enjoyed a considerable influence over the monastic milieus of Egypt and Palestine, his writings were probably read and defended by many monks, among whom we could count Jerome and his monastery.[171]

Familiarity with Epiphanius's writings may have put Jerome on edge with regard to other heresies that were becoming widespread in monastic milieus—like that of Rufinus—in which Origen was avidly studied, such as the belief that man lost the image of God after the Fall, or that in the resurrection we will have completely spiritual bodies in which the outward biological distinctions between male and female will entirely disappear, in flat opposition to the Apostle's Creed of the Roman Church, which has always confessed a resurrection of the *flesh*—*carnis resurrectionem*.

It was the last of these, the denial of the resurrection of the flesh, that seems to have disturbed Jerome most, for he probably came to understand that belief in the eschatological obliteration of all bodily distinction between man and woman must needs have consequences for the way man and woman lived and behaved toward their bodies in the present age. Origen himself was a conspicuous example: perhaps his decision to castrate himself was related to, if not influenced by, his belief that in the age to come he would be lacking the bodily members he had chosen to amputate. But, more important still, Jerome understood that the denial of the resurrection of the flesh undermined belief in the Resurrection of Christ, and therefore jeopardized the whole foundation of Christian faith.

Jerome informs us that this denial of the resurrection of the flesh was at the heart of a clandestine sect of followers of Origen in and around Jerusalem which had John, the Bishop of Jerusalem, and Rufinus as figureheads.[172] Although they never professed such a clearly heretical position openly, they developed a whole code of ambiguous language by which they could *appear* to believe in the resurrection of the flesh while in actual fact they denied it. Many believers, who could not make heads or tails of these subtle theological distinctions, were successfully deceived by their astuteness. But Jerome, a far more intelligent believer, found such ambiguity intolerable, and he quickly developed an antagonism not only to Origen, but also to his deceptive devotees who wanted to "have their cake and eat it too," i.e., to profess the heretical teachings of Origen *and* be accepted as fully orthodox Catholics. Fearing that association with this group, and even Rufinus, would jeopardize his own faith, he preferred to separate himself from them, in accordance with the words of Christ from the Gospel of Matthew (18:2) that if one's hand, foot or eye should lead him into sin, he should cut it off and cast it away. Jerome, commenting on this passage, would state:

> Therefore, let every affection be cut off, and every close relation amputated, lest on the grounds of religion any of the faithful suffer scandal. If, he says, someone is so closely connected to you as hand, foot or eye, and is beneficial and attentive, and keenly perceptive, but, nevertheless, causes you scandal, and through inharmonious lifestyle leads you into hell: it is better, nevertheless, that you be deprived of his closeness and the advantages of the flesh that he procures for you, lest, as you seek to save your relatives and friends, you have cause for ruin.[173]

The scene was thus set for Jerome to cross the figurative Rubicon, and distance himself publicly and definitively from Origen and his writings.

The occasion for him to do so was the appearance in Palestine in 393 of a certain monk named Atarbius, who, perhaps under the influence of Epiphanius's writings, started something of a crusade against Origen. Since both Jerome and Rufinus were known to be long-time admirers of the Alexandrian theologian, he made it a point to interview them both, and sought to obtain from them a formal condemnation of Origen's heretical teachings. At this point, Jerome did not need to be asked twice to make such a pronouncement. But Rufinus entirely refused, and dodged Atarbius as much as he could lest he be forced to either denounce his beloved teacher, or appear to share his heretical views.[174] A rift was thus made between Jerome and Rufinus that, despite subsequent attempts at reconciliation, was never really bridged, but rather grew wider and wider with time.

Upon Atarbius's exit from the scene, Epiphanius now made his entrance into the growing crusade against Origen in Palestine. Around Easter of 394, he made a formal visit to the Church of the Holy Sepulchre in Jerusalem. Epiphanius also had become aware of the covert sect in Jerusalem, with its astutely ambiguous language denying the resurrection of the flesh, and set out to expose and denounce both it and Origen once and for all. Thus, he preached at length against the errors of Origen and openly called on John to condemn them. John, infuriated, yet wishing to preserve his reputation of orthodoxy, delivered his own lengthy sermon showcasing the orthodox beliefs he held, while failing to mention any of the Origenistic errors Epiphanius had accused him of holding. He accused Epiphanius, moreover, of holding the Anthropomorphite heresy, which attributes a human body and other human attributes to the uncreated, immutable, and solely spiritual divine essence. Epiphanius denied holding this belief, which Origenists typically hurled at anyone unfavorable to Origen, yet pressed John still more to renounce Origen, "the father of Arius and root of all heresies." Shortly after this momentous episode, Epiphanius was essentially driven not only out of the Church, but out of the city itself. He took refuge in Bethlehem, in Jerome's monastery, and there ensued a de facto break of communion between Epiphanius and Jerome's monastery and John and his clergy.

Epiphanius Tries to Lighten the Hardships of a Community

Though it seems matters couldn't get more convoluted in this controversy, they soon did. Before Atarbius and Epiphanius began their crusade against Origen, there seems to have been a good relationship between John, the Bishop of Jerusalem, and

Jerome's community. For some time, John thought Jerome's younger brother Paulinian would make a good priest, and tried on several occasions to ordain him, but to no avail.[175] The young man fled from this honor, either because he did not consider himself worthy of it, or considered it a burden and genuinely did not want it, or (it must be admitted) because that was a typical thing monks did, and avoiding the priestly office in this manner tended to make others regard them as all the worthier of the honor. Be that as it may, Paulinian consistently fled this honor from both John and other bishops as well.

One fine day, during a period when Epiphanius was residing near Bethlehem at his monastery in Eleutheropolis—which was *not* under the jurisdiction of the bishop of Jerusalem—Paulinian, accompanied by some deacons and other brothers of their monastery, paid Epiphanius a visit, apparently to make amends because they thought Epiphanius was disappointed with them over something.[176] Here it must be mentioned that Epiphanius was one of the bishops who wanted to ordain Paulinian to the priesthood. As, therefore, it was drawing near to the time for Mass, and Epiphanius saw Paulinian advancing toward the monastery, seeing this as a providential moment to accomplish his pious scheme, he relates that:

> I gave order by means of many Deacons to seize him—he being entirely oblivious and entertaining no suspicion whatsoever that this would happen— and commanded them to cover his mouth, lest perchance, desiring to escape, he should adjure us in the name of Christ. And first we ordained him a Deacon, setting before him the fear of God and compelling him to exercise the sacred ministry. He greatly persisted in crying out that he was

> unworthy, and saying that it was a heavy burden which exceeded his strength. We only barely, therefore, coerced him, and were able to persuade him with the witness of the Scriptures, and brought before him the commandments of God. And when he had ministered in the holy sacrifices, we then, again with great difficulty and holding his mouth, ordained him Priest: and we used the same words as before to persuade him, and urged him to sit among those of Priestly rank.[177]

Thus it was that Paulinian first heard the words *Tu es sacerdos in æternum secundum ordinem Melchisedek*— "You are a priest forever according to the order of Melchizedek."

Epiphanius continues:

> Then we wrote to the Priests of the monastery, and other brothers: and rebuked them as to why they had not written to us about him, since before that year I heard many of the brothers complain that they had nobody to consecrate the Eucharist for them, and they all with one accord asked him (i.e., Paulinian) to do it, and attested to the great benefit he would bring to the common good of the monastery.[178]

At this point, many a modern reader is probably scratching his or her head, because Epiphanius acknowledges that, while there were, indeed, priests in Jerome's monastery, nevertheless the brothers were complaining that there was nobody to offer the Eucharist for them. How does one make sense of these statements? Epiphanius tells us when explaining his reasons for imposing priestly ordination on Paulinian:

> While, indeed, I saw that a multitude of holy brothers dwelt in the monastery, and that the holy Priests Jerome and Vincent, on account of their reverent modesty and humility, wished not to perform the sacrifices that fall to their rank, and to labor in this part of the sacred ministry which constitutes the chief salvation of Christians . . .[179]

And in those few words, almost incidentally, Epiphanius not only relates a very interesting fact about St. Jerome—that he, along with his fellow priest-monk Vincent, habitually refrained from offering Mass—but also provides us with a remarkable witness of the great doctor's singular virtue in explaining why he refrained from offering the Eucharist—due to his reverent modesty and deep humility.

But neither this fact concerning St. Jerome, nor the fact that his brother Paulinian was forcibly ordained against his will, seemed to draw anyone's attention. Nobody contested the *validity* of Paulinian's ordination, but John of Jerusalem contested its *licitness*, for, he would argue, it concerned a monk in a monastery in Bethlehem, which fell under his jurisdiction. He thus argued that Epiphanius had committed a breach of Ecclesiastical Law, and exploited this apparent violation of jurisdiction to both avenge and conceal the humiliation he suffered when Epiphanius denounced him as a heretic. He must have also been jealous that he was not the one to have ordained Paulinian, for he issued a decree establishing that anyone who said that Paulinian was ordained a priest by Epiphanius would be prohibited from entering the churches in his diocese. Thenceforth Jerome and his monks could only glance at the cave of the Lord's Nativity from afar, while heretics wandered in and out of it.[180]

But John was not satisfied with administering this ill-treatment to Jerome and his monks. Though Epiphanius wrote him letters defending his ordination of Paulinian and denying any violation of Ecclesiastical norms, and, furthermore, indicating that the real reason for John's resentment lay in the fact that Epiphanius had denounced him as a heretic, John refused to respond to the old bishop monk.[181] He chose instead to appeal to Theophilus, the Bishop of Alexandria, asking him to intervene to chastise Jerome and bid him to observe the holy canons.

Archbishop Theophilus was a fascinating character. This successor of St. Athanasius and predecessor of St. Cyril, his nephew, on the patriarchal throne of Alexandria, played a remarkable role in the ecclesiastical politics of his time. As he had frequent interactions with the monks in Egypt, he is often mentioned in the *Apophthegmata Patrum*, and not a few sayings are attributed to him. The portrait these accounts paint of Theophilus is that of a man who did not initially understand the *raison d'etre* of monastic life, and therefore unwittingly meddled in the lives of the monks in vexing ways. With time, however, it seems that he came to understand and considerably appreciate their life and vocation. The virtue, therefore, that is most conspicuous in this great man is that of *docility*.[182]

We observe this docility at work in his dealings with St. Jerome. As he had no reason to doubt the truth of John of Jerusalem's complaint, he intervened in a subdued and respectful manner on his behalf. Jerome appreciated this approach, and responded in an important letter in which he praises Theophilus's prudent meekness, defends Epiphanius's ordination of Paulinian, and identifies the real reason for John's resentment to be the incident in the Church of the Holy Sepulcher, in which Epiphanius denounced John as a heretic.[183] Theophilus had called Jerome to make peace and be restored to communion with John. Jerome replies that it is not up to him to do this because the hostility resides with John, not with himself, and it is John who divides himself from the Church, and thus from Jerome, through his heretical beliefs, which entails a lack of charity. As he puts it:

> We neither split the Church, nor divide ourselves from communion with our forefathers: but from the very cribs of our infancy, if I may say so, we have been nourished on Catholic milk. No one is a greater man of the Church than he who was never a heretic. But we do not recognize peace without charity, nor communion without peace. We also read in the Gospel: *If you bring your gift to the altar, and there remember that your brother has something against you, leave your gift there before the altar, and go first to be reconciled with your brother; then come and offer your gift (Matt. 5:13, 24).* If we cannot make our offering without peace, how much the less can we accept the Body of Christ without it? In what state of conscience can I draw near to the Eucharist, and respond Amen, if I doubt the charity of the one who administers it to me?[184]

In this important passage, St. Jerome shows us that genuine Ecclesial communion is not mere absence of conflict or mutual acceptance between brothers; indeed, it also entails sharing the same faith as our forefathers in the Church, and thus authentic Ecclesial communion is inseparable from and depends upon holding the fullness of Catholic truth as it has been handed down through the ages. It is for this reason that Jerome could not receive Communion from John or his priests, for he doubted that they were in communion with the Church of all time—the Church triumphant—and this cannot but bring with it a lack of Christian charity. In the last words of this passage, moreover, Jerome clarifies for us, in accordance with the witness of St. Epiphanius discussed above, that his custom was to receive the Eucharist from the hands of other Priests, and not from his own hand in the context of a Mass at which he officiated, for he says, "In what state of conscience can I draw near to the Eucharist, and respond Amen, if I doubt the charity of the one who administers it to me?"

Theophilus, therefore, was initially favorable not only to John of Jerusalem, but also to the Origenists among the monks of Egypt. Perhaps the most striking evidence of this initial support for the Origenist position was a famous letter in which he condemned the heresy of Anthropomorphism, triumphantly remembered by St. John Cassian (a saint of orthodox belief who, like St. Jerome, appreciated the sound teachings and contributions of Origen) at the outset of his 10th conference. The letter upset many of the monks, however, who detected in Theophilus's argumentation a hint of that Origenist error that asserts man lost the image of God after the Fall. Thanks to the docility with which God had blessed him, however, and to the intervention of a saintly monk, Abba Aphou (known as Apphy in the *Apophthegmata*), Theophilus saw the danger of holding such a position,[185] and made a diametrical turn against Origen and his teaching, becoming Epiphanius's principal collaborator in the crusade against the heresies of Origen.

While John still had Theophilus's support, however, he also wrote letters to Rome denouncing Jerome and Epiphanius for Paulinus's "illicit" ordination. Word eventually got back to Jerome through Pammachius, who as his spiritual son and Paula's son-in-law, continued to conduct matters on their behalf in Rome, and asked Jerome to clarify the situation. It was thus that Jerome wrote his famous treatise against John of Jerusalem. Although he never finished the treatise, and in all likelihood never published it, it remains one of his important works. As it was his attempt to defend himself and Epiphanius in a very painful situation, this treatise contains a double dose of his satirical firepower, for he felt a pressing need to defend the Church and the truths of the Faith in addition to himself and his monastery. One of the most salient parts of the treatise is his defense of the Resurrection, a veritable treatise within the treatise which is one of the most eloquent expositions of the Church's faith in the true Resurrection of Christ. At the end of the treatise, moreover, he offers us yet further insights into the way he lived out his priesthood. In the midst of defending Epiphanius's ordination of his brother and arguing that his ordination is not the real cause of John's strife, Jerome says to John:

> If the discord arose not from a discrepancy of faith, but, as you assert, from Paulinian's ordination, what great foolishness is that which refuses to give an answer to those who want one, thereby strengthening their cause? Confess the faith; but respond, nonetheless, to that which is asked of you, so that it may be evident to all that this conflict is not about faith, but about the ordination. As long as you are interrogated about the faith and you keep silent, your opponent can say to you: This is not about the ordination, but about faith. If the cause of the discord is the ordination, you are foolish to keep silent when questioned about faith. If the discord is about

> faith, then it is foolish to pretend that it is about the ordination. When you say, moreover, that you asked that "they" be subject to the Church of God, and neither tear it apart, nor make a kingdom for themselves, I have no idea concerning whom you say this. If you meant myself and the Priest Vincent, you have been asleep for quite some time, for you say this now, 13 years after we settled in Bethlehem. Indeed, the reason I forsook Antioch and he Constantinople, both renowned cities, was not to praise your eloquent preaching among the people, but so that, weeping over the sins of our youth amidst the fields and the solitude of the desert, we might call down upon us the mercy of Christ. If, however, you were referring to Paulinian, know that he is subject to his bishop and living in Cyprus, and comes every now and then to visit us, not as one of your priests, but as that of another, i.e. of him who ordained him. But even if he desired to be here, and peacefully dwell in solitude partaking of our exile, what does he owe you if not the honor which we owe all bishops? Say that you ordained him: you would hear the same thing from him as that which the bishop Paulinus of blessed memory heard from me, a wretch of a man: "Did I ask you to be ordained? If in conferring the priesthood you do not deprive us of the monastic state, do as it seems best to you. But if by the title of priest you divest me of that on account of which I forsook the world, I keep that which I have always had: you sustained no losses in this ordination."[186]

What is clear from this passage is that St. Jerome regarded his monastic vocation as paramount in his life. Although he could have pursued a priestly career in the renowned city of Antioch, he chose to abandon such a course in favor of the monastic solitude he so desired. By doing so he proclaimed the primacy of the contemplative life over the active life, something which Christ Himself had established during His earthly life when saying that Martha's sister Mary had chosen the better part (cf. Luke 10: 42). As a monk, furthermore, he was strongly drawn to the penitential dimension of this calling and felt the need to weep for his sins, as so many desert monks had done before him, and so call down Christ's mercy not only on himself, but on Christ's whole mystical Body, of which he was a living member. From these life-giving sources of contemplation and compunction flowed those precious waters, his translations of the Scriptures and extensive commentaries on them. From the same streams sprang the diligent care he gave to souls, both those directly entrusted to his care, and also those who wrote to him from every corner of the globe seeking his spiritual guidance. And though there is an undeniably priestly character to all these activities, we can say that it was primarily in contemplation and compunction that he lived out the mystery of his priesthood, since, according to his own admission, he customarily refrained from administering the sacraments. There were probably many reasons for this, in addition to his attachment to the monastic life, and the rough sketch we have drawn of the ecclesiastical and doctrinal controversies in which he was immersed should suffice to indicate that the unpleasant dynamics of ecclesiastical politics probably played a role in his decision to refrain from active priestly service. The reason given by St. Epiphanius, however, is that he did not say Mass on account of his "reverent modesty and humility" (*propter verecundiam, et humilitatem*). That is to say, his reverence for the Holy Eucharist was so great that he did not deem himself to be a worthy minister of so august a sacrament, and, therefore, customarily received the Lord's Body as did the non-ordained members of Christ's flock. In doing so he was also being faithful to the principles distinguishing the monastic from the clerical state which he once delineated in his youthful letter to Heliodorus:

> The objective, however, of Monks, is different from that Clerics . . . Clerics feed the sheep: I am fed. They live from the altar: but mine is the fate of the barren tree, to whose base the ax is laid, if I fail to bring a gift to the altar.

If it was not so clear before, now perhaps we can see that the gifts which this monk felt so compelled to bring to the altar were precisely those of contemplation and compunction. There, time and time again, at the foot of the altar, he faithfully deposited these gifts, and thus was ever more disposed to receive that gift of gifts, the Eucharistic Body of Christ. And it is this dimension of St. Jerome's life, at once both humbling and inspiring, that probably moved some unknown soul to write the famous Medieval legend known as *De Morte Hieronymi*, which, in turn, inspired the artistic masterpieces of Botticelli and Domenichino, among others, which represented his last Communion. And though that memorable Communion was the last of St. Jerome in this life, it was merely the prelude of the eschatological banquet which he now fully enjoys, and to which his earthly life was ever directed, as can be seen in this lovely passage from his commentary on the Prophet Ezechiel:

Then shall they be led into their land—the land of those who truly live—from all the nations: and He will feed them on the peaks of Israel, concerning which David declares: "I lifted up my eyes unto the mountains, whence my help comes" (Ps. 120:1) . . . There shall they rest on verdant meadows and shall say: "The Lord feeds me, and nothing shall be wanting unto me: in wholesome pastures He shall settle me: He led me forth upon the waters of refreshment" (Ps. 22:1-2). And there they shall be fed upon the most abundant pastures of all Israel's mountains. We are given an infinite promise, and hope of beatitude, when the Lord assures us, saying: I shall feed my sheep; and shall entrust them by no means to wicked shepherds, and I shall make them lie down, says the Lord God, that they may rest in the bosom of Abraham, Isaac, and Jacob. Then that which had been lost among the Gentiles shall be sought: and that which went astray in the persuasion of the heretics shall be brought back: the injured and the ailing shall be strengthened; that what is written may be brought to pass: "Who heals all their infirmities, and bandages their injuries."[187]

EPILOGUE

HAVING GIVEN an account of the way St. Jerome lived out his priesthood, I would like to offer some thoughts on the enduring significance, albeit faint and indirect, of his example by considering two saints who resembled the doctor of Bethlehem in surprising ways.

The first is the "Poverello of Assisi," St. Francis, who passed from this life a just a few days after the anniversary of St. Jerome's passing, and like St. Jerome, nurtured a deep love for Christmas and Bethlehem, expressed above all in the famous episode of Greccio. Though Thomas of Celano's description of the event is deeply moving, it is also a bit long; we will, therefore, quote St. Bonaventure's account of the event, which, in addition to being moving in its own right, has the benefit of being concise:

> Three years before he died, St. Francis decided to celebrate the memory of the birth of the Child Jesus at Greccio, with the greatest possible solemnity. He asked and obtained the permission of the pope for the ceremony, so that he could not be accused of being an innovator, and then he had a crib prepared, with hay and an ox and an ass. The friars were all invited and the people came in crowds. The forest re-echoed with their voices and the night was lit up with a multitude of bright lights, while the beautiful music of God's praises added to the

> solemnity. The saint stood before the crib and his heart overflowed with tender compassion; he was bathed in tears but overcome with joy. The Mass was sung there and Francis, who was a deacon, sang the Gospel. Then he preached to the people about the birth of the poor King, whom he called the Babe of Bethlehem in his tender love. A knight called John from Grecio, a pious and truthful man who had abandoned his profession in the world for love of Christ and was a great friend of St. Francis, claimed that he saw a beautiful child asleep in the crib, and that St. Francis took it in his arms and seemed to wake it up.[188]

In this memorable account of the "Poverello's" love for the Child Jesus and Bethlehem we see gleam through, from centuries past, some salient aspects of St. Jerome's life: his love of poverty and the ascetic life, and his devotion to the mystery of Christmas. One aspect that remains unsaid, however, but which was present in the "Poverello's" life and thus numbers him among St. Jerome's spiritual descendants, was the deep reverence he had for the mystery of the Most Holy Eucharist. Due to this reverence, he refrained from being ordained a priest, considering himself unworthy of such a sublime ministry. This aspect of his life is highlighted by the second saint I would like to consider: St. Therese of the Child Jesus.

In a life as singularly magnanimous as hers, one could find ways in which she resembles many saints, as others before me have sought to point out. Nevertheless, the striking things she had in common with St. Jerome deserve to be mentioned. To begin with, she was deeply devoted to the Child Jesus, as her principal title as a Carmelite shows. She longed to enter Carmel on December 25, although this desire was never fulfilled. She passed from this life to eternity on September 30—the same day as St. Jerome's passing. She was steeped in the Scriptures, and like St. Jerome, thought in terms of and expressed herself by means of them, and would have loved to study them in the original languages and enlighten souls concerning them like the Prophets and Doctors. And yet, perhaps the most striking way in which she resembled the doctor of Bethlehem and saintly father of virgins becomes apparent in the memorable words she left us in Manuscript B:

> *I feel in me the vocation of* the PRIEST. With what love, O Jesus, I would carry You in my hands when, at my voice, You would come down from heaven. And with what love would I give you to souls!

At this point, we could say with St. Jerome, *Scimus ista*, that is, these words we know well. But don't stop there, and cleverly omit the rest of what she said:

> But alas! while desiring to be a *Priest*, I admire and envy the humility of St. Francis of Assisi and I feel the *vocation* of imitating him in refusing the sublime dignity of the *Priesthood*.

One of St. Jerome's special missions was to incarnate both these vocations. In our day, when Christ's Priesthood is so often mistakenly reduced to an "administrative position" of power, prestige, and preeminence, we greatly need the humility that shone forth in the Little Flower of Lisieux, the Poverello of Assisi, and the Lion of Bethlehem.

Endnotes

Introduction

1 According to Prosper of Aquitaine (See his continuation of St. Jeome's *Chronicon*, PL 27, 715), St. Jerome passed from this life to eternal life on September 30, 423. Most modern scholars, however, with good reasons, place the year of his passing in 419 or 420.

2 See *The Metropolitan Museum of Art Bulletin*, Mar., 1915, Vol. 10, No. 3 (Mar., 1915), pp. 39+52-56 available at https://www.jstor.org/stable/3254048.

3 *Saint Jerome* by Regine and Madeleine Pernoud, Translated by Rosemary Sheed, The Macmillan Company: New York, 1962, p. 2.

Chapter 1: The Eucharist as Exegetical Key to Understanding Scripture

4 *Commentary on Ecclesiastes;* PL 23, 1039. Unless otherwse noted, all translations of Jerome and other patristic authorities are my own and have been taken from the editions of Migne's *Patrologia*, "PL" denoting the *Patrologia Latina* and "PG" denoting the *Patrologia Græca*.

Porro, quia caro Domini verus est cibus, et sanguis ejus verus est potus, juxta ἀναγωγήν, hoc solum habemus in præsenti sæculo bonum, si vescamur carne ejus, et cruore potemur, non solum in mysterio (Eucharistia), sed etiam in Scripturarum lectione. Verus enim cibus et potus, qui ex verbo

Since the flesh of the Lord is true food, and his blood is true drink, according to the anagogical sense, this alone is our good in the present age, if we are nourished by his flesh and drink his blood, not only in the mystery (Eucharist), but also in the reading of the Scriptures. Indeed, true food and drink

Dei sumitur, scientia Scripturarum est.

gathered from the Word of God is the knowledge of the Scriptures.

5 As will be seen further on when discussing the controversy with Jovinian, St. Jerome unambiguously maintains that union with Christ in sacramental Communion is greater than union with Him through prayer or meditation: *Quid est majus orare, an Corpus Christi accipere ? Utique accipere Corpus Christi.*

6 *Commentary on Matthew*, Book IV, Ch. XXVI, PL 26, 195.

Postquam typicum Pascha fuerat impletum, et agni carnes cum apostolis comederat, assumit panem, qui confortat cor hominis, et ad verum Paschæ transgreditur sacramentum, ut quomodo in præfiguratione ejus Melchisedech, summi Dei sacerdos, panem et vinum offerens fecerat (Genes. XIV), ipse quoque in veritate sui corporis et sanguinis repræsentaret.

After the figurative Passover had been fulfilled, and He had eaten the flesh of the lamb with His apostles, He takes bread, that strengthens the heart of man (cf. Ps. 103:15), and passes over to the sacrament of the true Passover, so that as Melchisedech, priest of God Most High, had done offering bread and wine as a type in anticipation of Him (cf. Gen. 14:18), He likewise should make the offering in the truth of His body and blood.

7 *Letter XXI to Damasus concerning the two sons*, 26; PL 22, 388.

Vitulus saginatus qui ad pœnitentis immolatur salutem, ipse Salvator est, cujus quotidie carne pascimur, cruore potamur.

The fatted calf which is slaughtered for the penitent's salvation is the Savior Himself, on whose flesh we daily feed, whose blood we drink.

8 *Commentary on Ezechiel*, Book XII, Ch. XLI; PL 25, 399.

Salvator quoque generis humani pascha fecit in cœnaculo, et magno latoque cœnaculo, atque omni sorde purgato stratoque, et ad spirituale convivium præparato, ubi mysterium corporis et sanguinis suis tradidit discipulis, et æternam nobis agni immaculati reliquit festivitatem.

The Savior of mankind also celebrated a Passover in a higher chamber, it too was a large and wide upper room, purged of all uncleanness and strewn, prepared for a spiritual banquet, where He bequeathed the mystery of His body and blood to His disciples, and left us the eternal festivity of the immaculate lamb.

9 *Commentary on Ezechiel*, Book XIII, Ch. XLIV; PL 25, 429.

Hæc igitur porta, quæ omnibus clausa est (vir enim non transibit per eam), erit clausa principi, sive duci, et illius adventu reserabitur, qui sedebit in ea, ut comedat panem coram Domino: de quo ipse in Evangelio profitetur, dicens: Meus cibus est ut faciam voluntatem ejus qui misit me, et compleam opus ejus (Joan. IV, 34). Ipse est princeps, et pontifex secundum ordinem Melchisedech, et hostia et sacerdos, qui in conspectu Patris nobiscum cœlestem comedit panem, et vinum bibit, de quo loquitur in Evangelio : Non bibam de genimine vitis hujus, nisi cum bibero illud novum in regno Patris mei (Matt. XXVI, 29) : in illo videlicet regno, de quo et ipse et alibi ait : Regnum Dei intra vos est (Luc. XVII, 21). Clausaque erit porta. Nemo enim potest passionis Domini, corporisque ejus et sanguinis pro majestate rei sacramenta cognoscere. Tantæque bonitatis est, et clementiæ princeps noster, ut cum solus sedeat in porta, quæ clausa est, et panem coram Domino comedat, velit mensæ suæ atque convivii plures habere consortes, et dicat: Ecce ego sto ad ostium et pulso; si quis aperuerit mihi, ingrediar ad eum et cœnabo cum illo, et ipse mecum (Apoc. III,20). Solus autem panem comedit coram Domino, quia substantia ejus divinaque natura a cunctis creaturarum

This door, therefore, which is closed to everyone (for no man shall pass through it), shall be closed to the prince, and to the duke, and shall be opened by the coming of Him who shall sit in it, that He might eat bread before the Lord: concerning which in the Gospel He Himself speaks openly, saying: My food is to do the will of Him who sent me, that I may accomplish His work (Jn. 4:34). He is the prince, and pontiff according to the order of Melchisedech, and victim and priest, who with us eats celestial bread in the Father's sight, and drinks the wine of which He speaks in the Gospel: I shall not drink of the fruit of this vine, if not when I drink it anew in My Father's kingdom (Mt. 26:29): in that kingdom, namely, concerning which He Himself says elsewhere: The kingdom of God is within you (Lk. 17:21). And the door shall be closed. Nobody, indeed, can know the sacraments of the Lord's passion, of His body and blood, on account of the majesty of the reality. And our Prince is of such goodness and clemency, that though He sits alone at the door, which is closed, He desires to have numerous companions at His table and banquet, and says: Behold, I stand at the door and knock; if someone should open to me, I shall enter near him and with

substantiis separata est. Ipse per eamdem vestibuli portam ingreditur et egreditur: quia et intus et foris, hoc est, infusus et circumfusus omnibus ; ingrediensque per portam, ut secum introducat eos, qui absque doctrina et ejus auxilio intrare non possunt; et egrediens, ut rursus alios introducat; et loquatur eis qui difficiliora non capiunt. Quod autem porta Orientalis extra terminos mundi semper clausa sit, et humano nequaquam pateat aspectui, Joannis Evangelium probat dicentis: Deum nemo vidit umquam: Unigenitus Filius qui est in sinu Patris, ipse enarravit (Joan. I, 18).

him dine, and he with me (Apoc. 3:20). Alone He eats bread before the Lord, for His substance and divine nature is distinct from all substances of creatures. He enters and exits through the same door of the atrium: for He is both within and without, that is, infused inside and surrounding everyone; and entering through the door, that with Himself He may lead in others, who without His teaching and assistance cannot enter; and exiting, that He may lead in others yet again; and speak to them who do not grasp the harder matters. But that the Eastern door beyond the limits of the world should be forever closed, and never be exposed to human sight, John's Gospel verifies when saying: No one has ever seen God: the only-begotten Son who is in the bosom of the Father, He has made Him known (Jn. 1:18).

10 *Commentary on Ezechiel,* Book XIV, Ch. XLV; PL 25, 455.

Et tollet, inquit, sacerdos de sanguine ejus, quod erit pro peccato omnium : qui aliis verbis agnus appellatur in Exodo, et in Evangelio, Baptista Joanne dicente : Ecce Agnus Dei, qui tollet peccata mundi (Joan. I,29). Sanguis autem ipse est pretiosus in quo redimur in passione Domini Salvatoris; cujus carnibus alimur, et cruore potamur.

And the priest shall take of its blood, which shall be for the sin of everyone: who in Exodus and in the Gospel by similar words is called a lamb, John the Baptist proclaiming: Behold the Lamb of God who takes away the sins of the world (Jn. 1:29). The blood, however, is that same precious blood by which we are redeemed in the passion of the Lord Savior; by whose flesh we are nourished, and whose blood we drink.

[11] *Commentary on Isaiah*, Book XV, Ch. LV; PL 24, 529-530.

Mirumque in modum emunt aquas absque pecunia; et non bibunt eas, sed comedunt. Ipse enim et aqua et panis est, qui de cœlo descendit (Joan. VI). Ergo quod in quibusdam exemplarisbus legitur : Emite, et bibite, ab imperitis scriptoribus immutatum est, qui putaverunt esse consequentius, si biberentur potius aquæ, quam comederentur. Est autem et pecunia pessima, sive argentum, quod reprobat Scriptura, dicens : Pecunia, quæ datur cum dolo, quasi testa reputabitur (Prov. XXVI, 23, sec. LXX); et in alio loco: Argentum vestrum reprobum (Jerem. VI, 30). Et est argentum quod Dei eloquiis comparatur: Eloquia Domini, eloquia casta: argentum igne examinatum terræ, purgatum septuplum (Ps. XI, 7). Spreto igitur illo argento et pecuniis, quibus aquas Domini emere non possumus, pergamus ad eum, qui tenens calicem Sacramenti, discipulis loquebatur: Accipite et bibite, hic est sanguis meus, qui pro vobis effundetur in remissionem peccatorum (Matt. XXVI, 27,28). Quod vinum miscuit et sapientia in cratere suo, omnes stultos sæculi mundique sapientiam non habentes, provocans ad bibendum: et ut non solum vinum emamus, sed et lac, quod significat innocentiam parvulorum, qui mos ac typus in Occidentis Ecclesiis hodie usque servatur, ut

What is more, in a wonderful manner they buy waters without money; and they do not drink them, but eat them. Indeed, He who came down from heaven, is both water and bread (Jn. 6). Thus, that which is read in some codices: Buy, and drink, was changed by uninformed scribes, who considered it more coherent that water should be drunk rather than eaten. There is, moreover, evil money, or silver, which the Scripture condemns when it says: Money which is given with deceit shall be reputed as a potsherd (Prov. 26:23 according to the Septuagint); and in another place: Your silver is condemned (Jer. 6:30). There is also silver which is compared to the words of God: The sayings of the Lord are pure sayings: silver tried by the fire, purified seven-fold (Ps. 11:7). Having thus rejected that silver and money with which we cannot purchase the waters of the Lord, let us press onwards to Him, who, holding the chalice of the Sacrament, spoke thus to His disciples: Receive and drink, this is my blood, which shall be shed unto the remission of sins (Mt. 26:27-28). This is the wine which Wisdom mixed in her bowl, inciting all the foolish ones, who lack the wisdom of this age and world, to drink. And we should purchase not wine alone, but also milk, which signifies

renatis in Christo vinum lacque tribuatur. De quo lacte dicebat et Paulus: Lac vobis potum dedi, non solidum cibum (I Cor. III,2). Et Petrus : Quasi modo nati parvuli, rationale lac desiderate (I Pet. II, 2). Unde et Moyses vinum et lac in Christi intelligens passione, mystico sermone testatur : Gratiosi oculi ejus a vino, et candidi dentes ejus a lacte (Genes. XLIX, 12). Pro lacte in præsenti loco LXX adipem transtulerunt. De quo sanctus David dicit in psalmo: Sicut adipe et pinquedine repleatur anima mea (Psal. LXII, 6) ; et in alio loco: Cibavit eos de adipe frumenti, et de petra melle saturavit eos (Psal. LXXX, 17). Qui adipes non aliud quam mysticam carnem sonant. Ad quam Dominus discipulos hortabatur, dicens : Nisi comederitis carnem meam, et biberitis sanguinem meum, non habebitis vitam in vobis (Joan. VI, 54).

the innocence of little ones, which custom and figure is kept to the present day in Western Churches, so that wine and milk are offered to those reborn in Christ. Concerning this milk Paul also used to say: I gave you milk to drink, not solid food (1 Cor. 3:2). And Peter: In the manner of new born babes, long for spiritual milk (1 Pt. 2:2). Hence Moses, also, understanding wine and milk as referring to Christ's passion, testifies with mystical words: His eyes are more lovely than wine, and His teeth are whiter than milk (Gen. 49:12). In place of "milk" here the Septuagint translated "fatness". Concerning this fatness saint David says in the Psalm: Let my soul be filled with fatness and grease (Ps. 62:6); and in another place: He fed them with fatness of wheat, and satisfied them with honey from the rock (Ps. 80:17). This fatness seems to be nothing other than the sacramental flesh to which the Lord summoned His disciples, saying: Unless you eat my flesh, and drink my blood, you will not have life within you (Jn. 6:54).

[12] *Commentary on Hosea*, Book III, Ch. XI; PL 25, 917

Et arbitrati sunt jugum meum leve, esse gravissimum : et declinavi ad eos deserens regna cœlorum, ut cum eis vescerer, assumpta forma hominis, sive dedi eis esum Corporis mei : ipse et cibus et conviva.

And they considered my light yoke to be terribly heavy: and I bowed down to them, deserting the heavenly realms, that I might eat with them, having assumed the form of man, and gave to them the food of my Body, which is both food and shared rejoicing.

13 *Commentary on Matthew*, Book II, Ch. XV; PL 26, 111-112.

Non vult eos Jesus dimittere jejunos, ne deficiant in via. Periclitatur ergo, qui sine cœlesti pane ad optatam mansionem pervenire festinat. Unde et angelus loquitur ad Eliam: *Surge, et manduca, quia grandem viam ambulaturus es (III Reg. XIX, 7).*

Jesus does not wish to send them away hungry, lest they faint on the way. Whoever, therefore, hastens to reach the desired dwellling place without the heavenly bread is in peril. Hence the angel also says to Elijah: *Rise, and eat, for you are setting out on a great journey (3 Kings 19:7).*

14 Sumunt boni, sumunt mali: sorte tamen inæquali, vitæ vel interitus. Mors est malis, vita bonis: vide, paris sumptionis quam sit dispar exitus.

15 *Adversus Jovinianum*, Book II; PL 23, 321.

Una est in mysteriis sanctificatio, Domini et servi, nobilis et ignobilis, regis et militis : quamquam pro accipientium meritis diversum fiat quod unum est. *Qui enim indigne manducaverit et biberit, reus erit violati Corporis et Sanguinis Christi (I Cor. XI, 27).* Numquid quia et Judas de eodem calice bibit, de quo et cæteri Apostoli, unius cum reliquis erit meriti ?

The sanctification in the sacraments is one for master and servant, nobleman and commoner, king and soldier: though that which is one may be differentiated according to the merits of the recipient. *He, indeed, who unworthily eats and drinks, will be answerable for the desecrated Body and Blood of Christ (1 Cor. 11:27).* Or do you suppose that since Judas, too, drinks from the same chalice as the other Apostles, he will deserve the same merit with the rest?

16 Lev. 22:14. This passage will be considered more in-depth further on.

17 *Dialogus adversus Pelagianos*, Book I, 34; PL 23, 529.

Ad extremum dicitur. *Si comederit homo de sanctificatis per ignorantiam, imputatur ei iniquitas atque delictum, et voti reus erit.* Unde et Apostolus monet Eucharisitam Domini cum cautione sumendam, ne in condemnationem nobis sumamus atque judicium (I Cor.

Finally it says: *If someone eateth of the sanctified things through ignorance, injustice and transgression is imputed to him, and he shall be answerable for the burnt-offering.* Hence the Apostle also admonishes that the Eucharist of the Lord is to be eaten with caution, lest we

XI). Si damnatur in lege ignorantia, quanto magis in Evangelio conscientia!

eat it unto our condemnation and judgment (1 Cor. 11:27). If ignorance is condemned in the law, how much more full knowledge in the Gospel!

Chapter 2: What it Means to Receive the Eucharist Worthily

[18] *Dialogus adversus Pelegianos,* Book III; PL 23, 585.

Panem quotidianum, sive, *super omnes substantias,* venturum Apostoli deprecantur, ut digni sint assumptione corporis Christi. Et vos per nimiam sanctitatem, securamque justitiam audacter vobis cœlestia dona vendicatis. Sequitur: *Dimitte nobis debita nostra, sicut et nos dimittimus debitoribus nostris.* De baptismatis fonte surgentes, et regenerati in Dominum Salvatorem, impleto illo, quod de se scriptum est: *Beati quorum remissæ sunt iniquitates, et quorum tecta sunt peccata (Ps. XXXI, 1),* statim in prima communione corporis Christi dicunt: *Et dimitte nobis debita nostra,* quæ illis fuerant in Christi confessione dimissa; et tu arrogans et superbus de sanctarum puritate manuum, et munditia eloquii gloriaris. Quamvis sit hominis perfecta conversio, et post vitia atque peccata virtutum plena possessio, numquid possunt sic esse sine vitio, quomodo illi, qui statim de Christi fonte procedunt? Et tamen jubentur dicere: *Dimitte*

The Apostles pray for the forthcoming *bread* that is *daily* or *above all substances,* that they might be worthy of the reception of the body of Christ. Whereas you, through abundant holiness and confident uprightness, audaciously arrogate to yourselves the heavenly gifts. Thereupon follows: *Forgive us our debts, as we also forgive our debtors.* Those rising up from the baptismal font, and born anew into the Lord Savior, fulfilling that which is written concerning them: *Blessed are they whose injustices are remitted, and whose sins are covered (Ps. 31:1),* immediately, when making their first communion with the body of Christ say: *And forgive us our debts,* debts which were already forgiven in the confession of Christ; whereas you are arrogant and proud owing to the purity of your holy hands, and glory in the refinement of your speech. However perfect be the conversion of a man, and complete his possession of virtues after vices

nobis debita nostra, sicut et nos dimittus debitoribus nostris (Matth. VI, 13): non humilitatis mendacio, ut tu interpretaris, sed pavore fragilitatis humanæ suam conscientiam formidantis.

and sins, can such people be as free of vice as those who immediately proceed from the font of Christ? And yet they are commanded to say: *Forgive us our debts, as we also forgive our debtors (Mt. 6:13)*: not in false humility, as you construe, but in the trembling of someone dreading his awareness of human fragility.

19 *καὶ ἄνθρωπος, ὃς ἂν φάγῃ ἅγια κατὰ ἄγνοιαν, καὶ προσθήσει τὸ ἐπίπεμπτον αὐτοῦ ἐπ'αὐτὸ καὶ δώσει τῷ ἱερεῖ τὸ ἅγιον.*

20 Leviticus 22:10-14:

Omnis alienigena non comedet de sanctificatis, inquilinus sacerdotis et mercenarius non vescentur ex eis. Quem autem sacerdos emerit, et qui vernaculus domus ejus fuerit : hi comedent ex eis. Si filia sacerdotis cuilibet ex populo nupta fuerit ad domum patris sui : de his quæ sanctificata sunt, et de primitiis non vescetur. Sin autem vidua, vel repudiata, et absque liberis reversa fuerit ad domum patris sui: sicut puella consueverat, aletur cibis patris sui. Omnis alienigena comedendi ex eis non habet potestatem. Qui comederit de sanctificatis per ignorantiam, addet quintam partem cum eo quod comedit, et dabit sacerdoti in sanctuarium (St. Jerome : ...ignorantiam, imputatur ei iniquitas atque delictum, et voti **reus erit**;). I Cor 11 :27 : Itaque quicumque manducaverit panem hunc, vel biberit calicem Domini indigne, **reus erit** corporis et sanguinis Domini

[10] No stranger shall eat of the sanctified things: a sojourner of the priests, or a hired servant shall not eat of them. But he whom the priest hath bought, and he that is his servant, born in his house, these shall eat of them. If the daughter of the priest be married to any of the people, she shall not eat of those things that are sanctified, nor of the firstfruits. But if she be a widow, or divorced, and having no children return to her father's house, she shall eat of her father's meats, as she was wont to do when she was a maid. No stranger hath leave to eat of them. He that eateth of the sanctified things through ignorance, shall add the fifth part with that which he ate, and shall give it to the priest into the sanctuary (St. Jerome: ...ignorance, injustice and transgression is imputed to him, and he **shall be answerable** for the burnt-offering). 1 Cor. 11:27: Therefore, whosoever shall eat this

bread, or drink the chalice of the Lord unworthily, shall be **guilty of (or answerable for)** the body and of the blood of the Lord.

21 In his commentary on the Gospel of Matthew (PL 26, col. 68), St. Jerome explains how this passage is ultimately about putting our love in order:

Qui amat patrem aut matrem plus quam me, non est me dignus. Et qui amat filium aut filiam super me, non est me dignus. Qui ante præmiserat : *Non veni pacem mittere super terram, sed gladium;* et dividere homines adversum patrem et matrem, et socrum, ne quis pietatem religioni anteferret, subjecit dicens : *Qui amat patrem aut matrem plus quam me.* Et in Cantico legimus Canticorum : *Ordinate in me charitatem (Cant. II,4).* Hic ordo in omni affectu necessarius est. Ama post Deum patrem, ama matrem, ama filios. Si autem necessitas venerit, ut amor parentum ac filiorum Dei amori comparetur, et non possit utrumque servari, odium in suos, pietas in Deum sit. Non ergo prohibuit amare patrem aut matrem, sed signanter addidit: *Qui amat patrem aut matrem plus quam me.*

He who loves father or mother more than me is not worthy of me. And whosoever loves son or daughter more than me, is not worthy of me. He who before had laid down: *I did not come to bring peace upon earth, but, rather, a sword;* and divide men from father and mother, and mother-in-law, lest someone should value the piety shown towards relatives more than the piety owed to God, he added: *He who loves father or mother more than me.* And in the Canticle of Canticles we read: *Order charity within me (Cant. 2:4).* This order is necessary in all love. Love your father and mother and children after God. If the force of circumstance should set the love of parents or children side by side with the love of God such that they mutually exclude each other, let hate be shown to your kin, but piety preserved unto God. He did not, therefore, forbid loving father or mother, but qualified this love by adding: *He who loves father or mother more than me.*

22 cf. *Epistola XXII to Eustochium*, 30; PL 22, 416.

23 The Greek of St. Athanasius clarifies what is ambiguous in the Latin translation: it is our love *for* or *towards* Christ *(εἰς Χριστὸν)* that is to be preferred. *Vita S. Antonii*, 14; PG 26, 865.

Χάριν τε ἐν τῷ λαλεῖν ἐδίδου τῷ Ἀντωνίῳ· καὶ οὕτω πολλοὺς μὲν λυπουμένους παρεμυθεῖτο, ἄλλους δὲ μαχομένους διήλλαττεν είς φιλίαν· πᾶσιν ἐπιλέγων μηδὲν τῶν ἐν τῷ κόσμῳ προκρίνειν τῆς εἰς Χριστὸν ἀγάπης.

Gratiam item Antonio loquenti dederat Dominus; ut mœstos plurimos consolaretur: concertantes alios reduceret in amicitiam, hortans omnes ut nihil mundanarum rerum anteferrent charitati Christi.

here is the translation of Evagrius of the same passage:

Sermo ejus sale conditus consolabatur mœstos, docebat inscios, concordabat iratos: omnibus suadens nihil amori Christi anteponendendum.

[24] St. Cyprian of Carthage, *Liber de Oratione Dominica,* XV. PL 4, col. 529.

Voluntas autem Dei est quam Christus et fecit et docuit. Humilitas in conversatione, stabilita in fide, verecundia in verbis, in factis justitia, in operibus misericordia, in moribus disciplina, injuriam facere non nosse, et factam posse tolerare, cum fratribus pacem tenere; Deum toto corde diligere, amare in illo quod Pater est, timere quod Deus est; Christo nihil omnino præponere, quia nec nobis quicquam ille præposuit ; charitati ejus inseparabiliter adhærere, cruci ejus fortiter ac fidenter assistere ; quando de ejus nomine et honore certamen est, exhibere in sermone constantiam, qua confitemur, in quæstione fiduciam, qua congredimur, in morte patientiam, qua coronamur. Hoc est cohæredem Christi esse velle, hoc est præcep-

The will of God is that which Christ both accomplished and taught. Humility in one's way of life, which is established in faith; modesty in words; justice in actions; mercy in works; discipline in behavior; to commit no injustice, yet to bear it when suffered. To be at peace with the brethren. To love God with all one's heart, loving Him as Father, yet fearing Him as God; to prefer nothing whatsoever to Christ, for neither did He prefer anything to us; to cling inseparably to His love, to attend to His Cross with fortitude and faithfulness. In whatever combat there may be concerning His name and honor, to display in word the constancy we profess, trust in the trial we encounter, in death the patience by which we are crowned. This is to

tum Dei facere, hoc est voluntatem Patris adimplere.

desire to be a co-heir with Christ, this is to accomplish the precept of God, this is to fulfill the will of the Father.

25 St. Augustine, *Letter LIV to Januarius*, 7-8; PL 33, 205.

Liquido apparet, quando primum acceperunt discipuli corpus et sanguinem Domini, non eos accepisse jejunos. Numquid tamen propterea calumniandum est universæ Ecclesiæ quod a jejunis semper accipitur ? Ex hoc enim placuit Spiritui sancto, ut in honorem tanti Sacramenti in os Christiani prius Dominicum corpus intraret, quam cæteri cibi: nam ideo per universum orbem mos iste servatur.

It is evident that when the disciples first received the body and blood of the Lord, they did not do so fasting. However, is the universal Church to be censured for the fact that now it is always received fasting? Indeed, it so pleased the Holy Ghost that in honor of such a Sacrament, the body of the Lord should enter the Christian's mouth before any other food: surely on that account this custom is observed throughout the entire world.

26 *Letter LXXI to Lucinium*, 6; PL 22, 672.

De Sabbato quod quæris, utrum jejunandum sit: et de Eucharistia, an accipienda quotidie, quod Romana Ecclesia et Hispaniæ observare perhibentur, scripsit quidem et Hippolytus vir disertissimus; et carptim diversi Scriptores e variis auctoribus edidere. Sed ego illud breviter te admonendum puto, traditiones Ecclesiasticas (præsertim quæ fidei non officiant) ita observandas, ut a majoribus traditæ sunt: nec aliorum consuetudinem, aliorum contrario more subverti. Atque utinam omni tempore jejunare possimus, quod in Actibus Apostolorum diebus Pentecostes et die Dominico, Apostolum Paulum, et cum eo credentes fecisse

As to your questions, the very eloquent man Hippolytus and other writers have written regarding the things that you inquired of me: whether or not one should fast on Saturday, and whether the Eucharist should be received daily, as is the custom in the Churches of Rome and Spain.

But I think I should counsel you by saying that Ecclesiastical traditions (especially those that do not hinder faith) are to be observed in the manner in which they have been handed down from our forebears, and that the custom of some is not to be overthrown by the contrary custom of others. Moreover, it would be great if we could fast

legimus (Act. 13.20.21). Nec tamen Manichææ hæreseos accusandi sunt, cum carnalis cibus præferri non debuerit spirituali. Eucharistiam quoque absque condemnatione nostri, et pungente conscientia, semper accipere, et Psalmistam audire dicentem: *Gustate et videte, quoniam suavis est Dominus (Psal. 33.9)*, et cum eo canere: *Eructavit cor meum verbum bonum (Psal. 44.1)*. Nec hoc dico, quod diebus festis jejunandum putem; et contextas quinquaginta diebus ferias auferam: sed unaquæque provincia abundet in sensu suo, et præcepta majorum, leges Apostolicas arbitretur.

at all times, as we read in the Acts of the Apostles that the Apostle Paul and those who were with him did in Paschaltide and on Sunday (Acts 13;20;21). Yet they are not to be accused of the Manichean heresy, since carnal food should not be preferred to spiritual food. The Eucharist as well, so long as it is not to our condemnation and without pang of conscience, is always to be received, so that we can hear the Psalmist saying: *Taste and see how good the Lord is (Psal. 33:9)*, and sing with him: *My heart hath brought forth a good word (Psal. 44:1)*. But neither do I affirm that we should fast on feast days, nor that we should eliminate the established festivities of the fifty days of Paschaltide. Rather, let each region abound in its own sense, and diligently examine the precepts of our forebears and the Apostolic laws.

27 The passage that is unrelated to the Eucharistic fast, Acts 21:24, depicts St. Paul observing a ritual fast during Paschaltide at the request of St. James and the other Apostles in Jerusalem, in order to win over the Jews who believed in Christ but were still attached to the Old Law, in accordance with what he says in 1 Cor. 9:20-21: *And I became to the Jews, a Jew, that I might gain the Jews: to them that are under the law, as if I were under the law (whereas myself was not under the law), that I might gain them that were under the law.*

28 Cf. *The Acts of the Apostles: Text and Commentary* by Giuseppe Riciotti, trans. Laurence Byrne, C.R.L., The Bruce Publishing Company, Milwaukee, 1958, p. 194: "**As they ministered,** λειτουργούντων αὐτῶν. **They** refers to the prophets and teachers and the others previously named, but it necessarily includes the Christian community which participated in the liturgy. It is not

stated in what the liturgy consisted, but in the episode of 20:7-11, it is specified that in the gathering at Troas, Paul **broke bread** and gave a long discourse. Everything inclines one to believe that in this meeting also at Antioch, the "breaking of bread" took place, and one or two discourses were given, probably by persons gifted with "charisms." It is important to explain that the term **liturgy** in Greek, and its derivatives (**liturgical, to follow the liturgy, etc.**), are found in the New Testament only in Luke and in the writings of his master, Paul. The Liturgy here is addressed **to the Lord, namely** Jesus Christ. In fact, **the chalice of benediction... is the Communion of the blood of Christ,** just as **the bread we break...is the partaking of the body of the Lord** (1 Cor. 10:16). It is worth noticing here that fasting is linked with the liturgy.

29 *The Acts of the Apostles: Text and Commentary*, p. 317.

30 A reference to the practice then observed in Rome and elsewhere in which the faithful reserved the Eucharist at their homes so as to communicate daily.

31 St. Bede the Venerable would later borrow Jerome's words "*quotiescumque uxori debitum reddo, orare non possum*" in his commentary on 1 Peter 3:7, then summarize the rest of the argument from Jerome's letter to Pammachius: *Quod si juxta alium apostoli sermonem sine intermissione orandum est, nunquam ergo mihi conjugio serviendum est, ne ab oratione cui semper insistere jubeor, ulla hora præpediar*" (cf. PL 93, 55).

Letter XLVIII to Pammachius, 15, in defense his writings against Jovinianum; PL 22, 505-506. The letter was written in the year 393.

Tumeant contra me mariti, quare dixerim : «Oro te, quale illud bonum est, quod orare prohibet: quod Corpus Christi accipere non permittit? Quando impleo mariti officium, non impleo continentis.» Jubet idem Apostolus in alio loco, ut semper oremus (1 Thess. 5). «Si semper orandum est, nunquam ergo conjugio serviendum. Quoniam quotiescumque uxori debitum reddo, orare non pos-

Let married men swell with anger against me for having said: « I ask you, what good is that which hinders prayer: which does not permit me to receive the Body of Christ? When I fulfill the duty of husband, I cannot fulfill that of the continent person. » The Apostle commands the same thing in another place—that we pray always (1 Thes. 5:17). « If we are always to pray, the duty of wedlock is never to be kept. For

sum.» Hoc quare dixerim, perspicuum est, quia interpretabar illud Apostoli dictum: *Nolite fraudare invicem, nisi forte ex consensu ad tempus, ut vacetis orationi (1 Cor. 7.5)*. Paulus Apostolus dicit, quando coimus cum uxoribus, nos orare non posse. Si per coitum quod minus est impeditur, id est, orare: quanto plus quod majus est, id est, Corpus Christi prohibetur accipere ? Petrus ad continentiam hortatur: *Ne impediantur orationes (1 Pet. 3.7)* nostræ. Quod hic, quæso, peccatum meum est? Quid commerui? Quid deliqui? Si turbidæ, et nebulosæ aquæ fluunt, non est alvei culpa, sed fontis. An idcirco arguor, quod de meo ausus sum adjicere : «Quale illud bonum est, quod Corpus Christi accipere non permittit ?» Ad hoc breviter respondebo. Quid est majus orare, an Corpus Christi accipere? Utique accipere Corpus Christi. Si per coitum quod minus est impeditur, multo magis quod majus est. Diximus in eodem volumine. Panes propositionis ex Lege non potuisse comedere David, et socios ejus nisi se triduo mundos a mulieribus respondissent (1. Reg. 21), non utique a meretricibus, quod damnatur a lege: sed ab uxoribus, quibus licite jungebantur. Populum quoque quando accepturus erat Legem in Monte Sina, tribus diebus jussum esse ab uxoribus abstinere (Exod. 19). Scio Romæ hanc esse

as often as I pay the debt to my wife, I cannot pray. » The reason I said this is clear, for I was interpreting that saying of the Apostle: *Do not deprive each other, except perchance for a time by mutual consent, that you may devote yourselves to prayer (1 Cor. 7:5)*. The Apostle Paul says that when we copulate with our wives we cannot pray. If by means of the conjugal act that which is less is hindered, that is, to pray: how much more is that which is greater hindered, that is, to receive the Body of Christ? Peter encourages abstinence: *Lest* our *prayers be impeded (1 Pt. 3:7)*. What, I ask, is my sin in this? Of what have I become guilty? What fault have I committed? If the waters that flow are muddy and dark, it is not the canal's fault, but that of the source. Or am I censured for the fact that I dared to add on my own: «What good is that which does not allow me to receive the Body of Christ? » To this I briefly respond. What is greater, to pray, or to receive the Body of Christ? Certainly, to receive the Body of Christ. If through the conjugal act that which is less is hindered, much more is that which is greater hindered. We stated in the same volume that David and his companions were prohibited by the law to eat the loaves of proposition unless they acknowledged themselves to have abstained from women for

consuetudinem, ut fideles semper Christi corpus accipiant, quod nec reprehendo, nec probo : *Unusquisque enim in suo sensu abundet (Rom. 14)*. Sed ipsorum conscientiam convenio, qui eodem die post coitum communicant, et juxta Persium, *noctem flumine purgant (Satyr. 2)* ; quare ad Martyres ire non audent ? quare non ingrediuntur Ecclesias? An alius in publico, alius in domo Christus est? Quod in Ecclesia non licet, nec domi licet. Nihil Deo clausum est, et tenebræ quoque lucent apud Deum. Probet se unusquisque, et sic ad Corpus Christi accedat; non quod dilatæ communionis unus dies, aut biduum sanctiorem efficiat Christianum, ut quod hodie non merui, cras vel perendie merear: sed quod dum doleo me, non communicasse Corpori Christi, abstineam me paulisper ab uxoris amplexu : ut amori conjugis, amorem Christi præferam. Durum est, et non ferendum est. Quis hoc sæcularium sustinere potest ? Qui potest sustinere, sustineat : qui non potest, ipse viderit. Nobis curæ est, NON QUID UNUSQUISQUE POSSIT, aut velit ; sed quid Scripturæ præcipiant, dicere.

three days (1 Kings 21), not—to be sure, from prostitutes, which is condemned by the law, but from their wives, to whom they could be lawfully united. Also, the people about to receive the Law on Mount Sinai were commanded to abstain from their wives for three days (Exodus 19). I know that at Rome it is the custom that the faithful always receive Christ's body, something which I neither reprehend nor commend. *Let each one abound in his own understanding (Rom. 14)*. But I address myself to the conscience of those who, after intercourse, communicate in the same day, and, according to Persius, *purify the night in the stream (Satyr. 2)*. Why don't they dare to go to the Martyrs? Why don't they enter the Churches? Is Christ one in public and another at home? What is not allowed in Church is neither allowed at home. Nothing is hidden from God, and even darkness shines for Him. Let each one examine himself, and so draw near to the Body of Christ; not that delaying communion for a day or two makes a Christian any holier, so that what I did not deserve today I shall be worthy of tomorrow or the day after; but that, as I am afflicted with sorrow at not having communicated with the Body of Christ, I might deny myself my wife's embrace, so that I may prefer the love of Christ to the

love of my spouse. "It is hard, insufferable," you will say. "What lay person can bear this?" Let him who can bear it bear it: let him who cannot see to it himself. Our concern is not to declare WHAT EACH MAN IS ABLE OR WILLING TO DO, but that which the Scriptures command.

32 c.f. Mt. 10:37: *He that loveth father or mother more than me is not worthy of me: and he that loveth son or daughter more than me is not worthy of me;* and Lk. 14:26: *If any man come to me, and hate not his father and mother and wife and children and brethren and sisters, yea and his own life also, he cannot be my disciple.*

33 *Commentary on Titus*, Ch. 1; PL 26, 568-569.

Sit autem episcopus et pudicus, quem Græci σώφρονα vocant: et Latinus interpres verbi ambiguitate deceptus, pro *pudico, prudentem* transtulit. Si autem laicis imperatur, ut propter orationem abstineant se ab uxorum coitu : quid de episcopo sentiendum est, qui quotidie pro suis populique peccatis, illibatas Deo oblaturus est victimas ? relegamus Regum libros, et inveniemus sacerdotem Abimelech de panis propositionis noluisse prius dare David et pueris ejus, nisi interrogaret, utrum mundi essent pueri a muliere: non utique aliena, sed conjuge (1 Reg. XI). Et nisi eos audisset ab heri et nudiustertius vacasse ab opere conjugali, nequaquam panes quos prius negaverat, concessisset. Tantum interest inter propositionis panes et corpus Christi, quantum inter umbram et corpora, inter imaginem et veritatem, inter ex-

A bishop should also be chaste, which the Greeks term σώφρονα: and which the Latin interpreter, deceived by the double meaning of the word, rendered *prudent*, rather than *chaste*. But if lay people are commanded to abstain from relations with their wives for the sake of prayer, what should we say about a bishop, who for his own sins and those of the people daily offers the unblemished sacrifices to God? Let us read again the books of Kings, and we shall find the priest Abimelech unwilling to give the show bread to David and his servants until he verified that the servants had been unpolluted by woman: and not, to be sure, by an unfamiliar woman, but by their wives (1 Kings 11). And unless he heard them affirm themselves to have abstained from marital relations for two days beforehand, he would not have conceded to give

emplaria futurorum et ea ipsa quæ per exemplaria præfigurabantur. Quomodo itaque mansuetudo, patientia, sobrietas, moderatio, abstinentia lucri, hospitalitas quoque et benignitas, præcipue esse debent in episcopo, et inter cunctos laicos eminentia : sic et castitas propria et (ut ita dixerim) pudicitia sacerdotalis, ut non solum ab opere se immundo abstineat, sed etiam a jactu oculi et cogitationis errore, mens Christi corpus confectura sit libera.

them the loaves which he had previously denied them. Such a gap exists between the show bread and the body of Christ as that which exists between bodies and their shadows, the truth and its image, the types of future realities and the realities themselves. To be sure, just as meekness, patience, sobriety, moderation, absence of profit, hospitality and benignity should all be outstanding in a bishop, and excelling that of lay people: so also chastity and modesty are properly priestly, so that he who is about [to] consecrate the body of Christ may have a mind unimpeded not only by impure works, but also by wandering eyes and wayward thoughs.

34 *Letter CXIV to Theophilus, 2;* PL 22, 934.

Mirati sumus in opere tuo utilitatem omnium Ecclesiarum, ut discant qui ignorant, eruditi testimoniis Scripturarum, qua debeant veneratione Sancta suscipere, et altaris Christi ministerio deservire; sacrosque calices, et sancta velamina, et cætera, quæ ad cultum Dominicæ pertinent Passionis, non quasi inania, et sensu carentia sanctimoniam non habere; sed ex consortio Corporis et Sanguinis Domini eadem qua Corpus ejus et Sanguis majestate veneranda.

We marveled at the benefit for all the Churches contained in your treatise, that by the evidence of the Scriptures, those who lack knowledge may learn how great the reverence should be with which we receive the Consecrated things, and zealously serve in the ministry at the altar of Christ; and how the sacred chalices and holy veils, and other items which pertain to the veneration of the Lord's Passion, are not to be regarded as superfluous and lacking meaning and empty of holiness; but rather, on account of their close association with the Body and Blood of the Lord are to be treated with the same august veneration as are His Body and Blood.

CHAPTER 3: JEROME'S EARLY LIFE AND MONASTIC VOCATION

35 Cf. Letter 8 to Chromatius, Jovinum and Eusebius, 4; PL 22, 340: *Scitis ipsi lubricum adolescentiæ iter, in quo et ego lapsus sum, et vos non sine timore transitis.*

36 Cf. *Commentary on Ezechiel*, Book 12, Ch. 4; PL 25, 375.

Dum essem Romæ puer, et liberalibus studiis erudirer, solebam cum cæteris ejusdem ætatis et propositi, diebus Dominicis sepulchra apostolorum et martyrum circuire; crebroque cryptas ingredi, quæ in terrarum profunda defossæ, ex utraque parte ingredientium per parietes habent corpora sepultorum, et ita obscura sunt omnia, ut propemodum illud propheticum compleatur: *Descendant ad infernum viventes (Ps. LIV,16).*	When I was a boy being formed by the liberal studies in Rome, in the company of peers who shared my purpose in life, I would visit the tombs of the Apostles and martyrs, and often enter the crypts which are burrowed into the depths of the earth, and contain in the walls on both sides of those entering the bodies of those there entombed. Such darkness pervades the whole scene that the prophetic verse is nearly fulfilled: *Let them go down alive into hell (Ps. 54:16).*

37 Cf. Letter II to Theodosium and the other anchorites; PL 22, 331: *Ego ita sum quasi a cuncto grege morbida aberrans ovis...Ego sum ille prodigus filius, qui omni, quam mihi pater crediderat, portione profusa, necdum me ad genitoris genua submisi.* See also Letter 18 to Damasus, PL 22, 363: *Qui peccator est, et mei similis, videt Dominum sedentem in valle Josaphat : non in colle, non in monte; sed in valle, et in valle judicii.*

38 Cf. Letter 5, to Florentius, PL 22, 337: *Interpretationem quoque Psalmorum Davidicorum, et prolixum valde de Synodis librum sancti Hilarii, quem ei apud Treviros manu mea ipse descripseram, ut mihi transferas peto.*

39 It is possible St. Jerome initially encountered the monastic movement during his student days in Rome, where it was first preached by St. Athanasius (cf. St. Jerome's letter to Principia, PL 22, 1089-1090), but as it was then seen by many Romans in a pejorative light, Jerome may not have been drawn to it then. However, St. Athanasius was also exiled in Trier during the years 335-337.

It seems Jerome's encounter with monasticism in Trier, around the year 367, was more favorable. Athanasius made monasticism famous in the West, not only through his *Vita Antonii* (a primitive Latin translation of which was in circulation shortly after the original was published) but also through his own preaching and teaching. Jerome mentions briefly his definitive response to a call to give his life to Christ in an early letter to Rufinus (*Letter III, 5;* PL 22, 334.), in which he erupts into the following lovely prayer in gratitude for his virtuous friend, admired mentor, and anticipated heavenly intercessor, Bonosus:

Gratias tibi, Domine Jesu, quod in die tua habeo, qui pro me te possit rogare. Scis ipse (tibi enim patent pectora singulorum, qui cordis arcana rimaris, qui tantæ bestiæ alvo inclusum Prophetam in profundo vides) ut ego, et ille pariter a tenera infantia ad florentem usque adoleverimus ætatem, ut iidem nos nutricum sinus, iidem amplexus foverint bajulorum: et cum post Romana studia ad Rheni semibarbaras ripas, eodem cibo, pari frueremur hospitio, ut ego primus cœperim velle te colere.

I give you thanks, Lord Jesus, that in that day of Yours, I should have someone to pray to you for me. You Yourself know (to you, indeed, the hearts of all are open, you who probe the secrets of the heart, who sees a Prophet in the depths enclosed within so great a monster's belly) that I and he from early infancy together grew into the bloom of young maturity, that we were nourished at the breasts of the same nurses, and carried in the arms of the same nannies: and that upon completing Roman studies, partook of the same food and dwelt in the same lodging when visiting the Rhine's half-civil banks, that there I first began to long to worship You.

See also *Adversus Jovinianum, Lib. I, 12;* PL 23, 228, where, commenting on Matthew 19:10, he sees consecrated celibacy as an act of divine worship, which Christ joyfully receives:

Libenter illos in meos sinus recipio, qui se castraverunt propter regna cælorum, et ob mei cultum noluerunt esse quod nati sunt.

With joy I take into my bosom those who have made themselves eunuchs for the kingdom of heaven, and for the sake of my worship, wished to forego their inborn instinct.

40 St. Heliodorus's memorial is kept by the Roman Martyrology on July 3.

41 Except Bonosus, who embraced the eremitical life on a desolate island in the Gulf of Quarnero, and Innocent who died of a fever shortly after the community was disbanded. As for the priest Evagrius, he may have accompanied Jerome for part of the way, but, in any case, arrived at his native city of Antioch and was already settled anew there when Jerome finally arrived.

42 Cf. *Letter 3 to Rufinus*, 3; PL 22, 333: *Nunc uno et toto mihi lumine Evagrio nostro fruor, cui ego semper infirmus ad laborem cumulus accessi.*

43 Cf. St. Basil, Letter 138 to Eusebius of Samosata as found in *The Fathers of the Church* series, trans. Sister Agnes Clare.

44 Cf. St. Jerome, Letter I to Innocent; PL 22, 331.

45 Cf. *Liber de Viris Illustribus, Caput CXXV*; PL 23, 711-714: *Evagrius, Antiochiæ episcopus, acris ac ferventis ingenii, cum adhuc esset presbyter, diversarum hypotheseon tractatus mihi legit, quos necdum edidit; Vitam quoque Beati Antonii de Græco Athanasii in sermonem nostrum transtulit.*

Also Letter 57 to Pammachius on the best manner of translating, PL 22, 572: *...in libro quo beati Antonii Vita describitur (Ex præfatione Evagrii ad Innocentium)...*

46 Cf. Letter 2 to Theodosius; PL 22, 331.

47 In letter 87 to Oceanus (PL 22, 696), which contains a poignant and lovely elegy for the recently deceased widow Fabiola, who died in the odor of sanctity, among other things Jerome recounts of her: *Librum quo Heliodorum quondam juvenis ad eremum cohortatus sum, tenebat memoriter; et Romana cernens mœnia, inclusam se esse plangebat; The book in which I, still a youth, bid Heliodorus come to the hermitage, she knew by heart; and seeing the walls of Rome, she wept at being incarcerated in them.* This second part is an allusion to one of the great lines of letter 14: *quamdiu te fumosarum urbium carcer includit? How long will the prison of smoky cities confine you?* (PL 22, 354).

48 *Letter 52 to Nepotianus*, 1-2; PL 22, 527-528.

Dum essem adolescens, imo pene puer, et primos impetus lascivientis ætatis eremi duritia refrenarem,

When I was coming of age, nay practically still yet a boy, and would curb the initial urges of

scripsi ad avunculum tuum sanctum Heliodorum exhortatoriam Epistolam, plenam lacrymis querimoniisque, et quæ deserti sodalis monstraret affectum. Sed in illo opere pro ætate tunc lusimus, et calentibus adhuc Rhetorum studiis atque doctrinis, quædam scholastico flore depinximus. Nunc jam cano capite, et arata rugis fronte, et ad instar bovum pendentibus a mento palearibus, *Frigidus obsistit circum præcordia sanguis (Virgil. Georg. Lib.* 2). Unde et in alio loco idem Poeta canit: *Omnia fert ætas, animum quoque.* Et post modicum: *Nunc oblita mihi tot carmina, vox quoque Mœrin Jam fugit ipsa (In ucol. Eclog. 8).* 2. Quod ne de Gentili tantum litteratura proferre videamur, divinorum voluminum sacramenta cognosce. David annos natus septuaginta, bellicosus quondam vir, senectute frigescente, non poterat calefieri. Quæritur itaque puella de universis finibus Israel Abisag Sunamitis, quæ cum rege dormiret, et senile corpus calefaceret *(3 Reg. 1).*

wanton youth with the desert's austerity, to your uncle, devout Heliodorus, I wrote an exhortative letter abounding in tears and complaints, which, in addition, displayed the affection of his forsaken companion. But in that work, on account of our age at that time we amused ourselves, and, still aflame with the studies and doctrines of orators, sketched out that piece with our scholarly best. Now, with a head of gray hair, and a forehead furrowed with wrinkles, and dewlaps like those of an ox sagging down from our chin, *Our cooled-off blood forms a wall round our heart (Virgil. Georg. Lib. 2).* Therefore, elsewhere the same Poet sings: *Old age robs you of everything, even your wits.* And a little further: *Now I've forgotten so many songs, and even my voice escapes me.* But lest we be seen to collect from pagan writings alone, consider the hidden realites of the sacred books. David at seventy years of age, though once a fiery warrior, with the onset of frigid old age couldn't keep himself warm. Therefore from every end of Israel a maiden is sought—Abisag the Sumamite—who would sleep near the king, to keep his elderly body warm (3 Kings 1).

49 From *The Bohairic Life of Pachomius*, in *Pachomian Koinonia, Volume One: The Life of Saint Pachomius and his disciples*, Cistercian Publications Inc., Kalamazoo, Michigan, 1980, pp. 51-52.

50 *The Sayings of the Desert Fathers*, Trans. Benedicta Ward, SLG Cistercian Publications, 1975, p. 99

51 *The Sayings of the Desert Fathers,* Trans. Benedicta Ward, SLG Cistercian Publications, 1975, p. 77

52 *The Sayings of the Desert Fathers,* Trans. Benedicta Ward, SLG Cistercian Publications, 1975, p. 144

53 See *Letter XIV, to Heliodorus, 8-9;* PL 22, 352-353.

8. Sed de hoc gradu pulsus, provocabis ad Clericos. An de his aliquid audeam dicere, qui certe in suis urbibus commorantur? Absit ut de his quidquam sinistrum loquar, quia Apostolico gradui succedentes, CHRISTI CORPUS sacro ore conficiunt; per quos et nos Christiani sumus. Qui claves regni cœlorum habentes, quodammodo ante judicii diem judicant: qui sponsam Domini sobria castitate conservant. Sed alia, ut ante perstrinxi, Monachorum est causa, alia Clericorum. Clerici pascunt oves: ego pascor. Illi de altario vivunt: mihi quasi infructuosæ arbori, securis ponitur ad radicem, si munus ad altare non defero. Nec possum obtendere paupertatem, cum in Evangelio anum viduam, duo, quæ sola sibi supererant, æra mittentem in gazophylacium, laudaverit Dominus *(Luc. 21.24).* Mihi ante presbyterum sedere non licet: illi, si peccavero, licet tradere me Satanæ in interitum carnis, ut spiritus salvus sit *(1 Cor. 5.5).* Et in veteri quidem Lege, quicumque Sacerdotibus non obtemperasset, aut etra castra positus, lapiabatur a populo ; aut gladio cervice subjecta, contemptum expiabat cruore *(Deut. 17.12).* Nunc vero

8. But displaced from this order (of monks), you will appeal to the Clerics. Shall I dare to say something about these, who without doubt dwell in their cities? Far be it from me to say something disparaging about them, for, succeding to the grade of the Apostles, they consecrate THE BODY OF CHRIST with holy words; thanks to them we also are made Christians. They possess the keys of the kingdom of heaven, and in some way judge us before the day of judgment. They safeguard the Lord's bride with sober chastity. The objective, however, of Monks, is different from that Clerics, as I intimated earlier. Clerics feed the sheep: I am fed. They live from the altar: but mine is the fate of the barren tree, to whose base the ax is laid, if I fail to bring a gift to the altar. And I cannot allege poverty as an excuse, when in the Gospel the Lord praised the old widow, who threw into the treasury the only two pennies she had (Lk. 21:24). I am not allowed to sit before a priest: to him, though, belongs the power to hand me over to Satan, should I sin, unto the destruction of my flesh, so that my spirit may be saved (1 Cor. 5:5). And in the

inobediens spirituali mucrone ore truncatur: aut ejectus de Ecclesia rabido dæmonum ore discerpitur. Quod si te quoque ad eumdem Ordinem pia fratrum blandimenta sollicitant, gaudebo de ascensu, sed timebo de lapsu.

old Law whoever did not obey the priests was either placed outside the camp or stoned by the people; or, with his neck to the sword exposed, would atone for his scorn with his own blood (Deut. 17:12). Now, indeed, the disobedient man is cut off by the edge of a spiritual sword: or, cast out of the Church, is mangled by the merciless mouth of demons. But if your brethren's pious flattery entice even you to the priestly Order, we shall rejoice at your promotion, but fear your fall.

Qui Episcopatum desiderat, bonum opus desiderat. Scimus ista: sed junge quod sequitur: *Oportet autem hujusmodi irreprehensibilem esse, unius uxoris virum, sobrium, pudicum, prudentem, ornatum, hospitalem, docibilem, non vinolentum, non percussorem, sed modestum (1 Tim. 3).* Et cæteris, quæ de eo sequuntur, explicitis, non minorem in tertio gradu adhibuit diligentiam, dicens : *Diaconos similiter pudicos: non bilingues, non multo vino deditos, non turpilucros: habentes ministerium fidei in conscientia pura. Et hi autem probentur primum: et sic ministrent, nullum crimen habentes.* Væ illi homini, qui vestem non habens nuptialem, ingreditur ad cœnam. Nihil superest, nisi statim audiat: *Amici quomodo huc intrasti?* Et illo obmutescente dicatur ministris: *Tollite illum, ligatis manibus et*

He who desires the Episcopacy desires a good work. These words we know well: but do not forget that which follows: *however such a one should be without reproach, the husband of one wife, sober, chaste, prudent, decorous, hospitable, docile, not given to wine, not violent, but modest (1 Tim. 3).* And having listed the other qualities that flow from these, he attaches no less assiduousness to those in the third degree of the priesthood, saying: *Deacons similarly should be chaste: not duplicitous, not given over to wine, not eager for deceitful gain, holding fast to the ministry of faith in a pure conscience. And let these be tried first, and only if they are guilty of no crime let them minister.* Woe to that man who, lacking the nuptial raiment, enters into the wedding feast. There is nothing left for him

pedibus, et mittite eum in tenebras exteriores, ubi erit fletus et stridor dentium (Matt. 22.12.13). Væ illi qui acceptum talentum in sudario ligans, cæteris lucra facientibus, id tantum quod acceperat, reservavit. Illico indignantis Domini clamore ferietur : Serve nequam, quare non dedisti pecuniam meam ad mensam; et ego veniens cum usuris exegissem eam (Matt. 35.16.17) ? Id est, deposuisses ad altare, quod ferre non poteras. Dum enim tu ignavus negotiator denarium tenes, alterius locum, qui pecuniam duplicare poterat, occupasti. Quamobrem sicuti qui bene ministrat, bonum gradum sibi acquirit : ita qui indigne ad calicem Domini accedit, reus erit Dominici Corporis et Sanguinis (1 Cor. 11).

but to hear straightway: *Friend, how did you get in here?* And he will be speechless, while the servants will be told: *Take him, and binding his hands and feet, throw him into the outer darkness, where there is wailing and gnashing of teeth (Mt. 22:12-13).* Woe to him who wraps the talent he received in a head band, and while the rest are earning profit, he saves nothing beyond that which he received. In that very place he shall be anguished by the outcry of his angry Lord: *Wicked servant, why did you not deposit my money at the bank; so that upon returning I should withdraw it with interest (Matt. 35:16-17)?* That is, you could have laid at the altar that which you were not able to bear. While you, a worthless businessman, hold back your money, you have idly occupied the post in which someone else could have doubled that money. For which reason, just as he who serves well wins for himself a good status: so he who unworthily draws near to the chalice of the Lord shall be answerable for the Body and Blood of the Lord (1 Cor. 11).

9. Non omnes Episcopi, Episcopi sunt. Attendis Petrum: sed et Judam considera. Stephanum suspicis : sed et Nicolaum respice, quem Dominus in Apocalypsi sua damnat sententia : qui tam turpia et nefanda commentus est, ut Ni-

9. Not all bishops are bishops. You behold Peter: but consider also Judas. You gaze at Stephen: look also at Nicolaitus, whom the Lord in the Apocalypse by his judgment condemns for having devised such disgraceful and nefarious things,

colaitarum hæresis ex illa radice nascatur. Probet se unusquisque, et sic accedat. NON FACIT Ecclesiastica dignitas Christianum. Cornelius Centurio adhuc ethnicus, dono Sancti Spiritus mundatur (Act. 10). Presbyteros Daniel puer judicat (Dan. 13): Amos ruborum mora distringens, repente Propheta effectus est. David pastor eligitur in Regem (1 Reg. 16). Minimum discipulum Jesus amat plurimum. Inferius frater accumbe, ut minore adveniente, sursum jubearis ascendere (Luc. 14). Super quem Dominus requiescit, nisi super humilem et quietum, et trementem verba sua (Isai. 66.2)? Cui plus creditur, plus ab eo exigitur. *Potentes potenter tormenta patientur (Sap. 6.7).* Nec sibi quisquam de corporis tantum mundi castitate supplaudat, cum omni verbum otiosum, quodcumque locuti fuerint homines, reddituri sint pro eo rationem in die judicii (Matt. 12.5) : cum etiam convicium in fratrem, homicidii sit reatus. Non est facile stare loco Pauli, tenere gradum Petri, jam cum Christo regnantium: ne forte veniat angelus, qui scindat velum templi tui, qui candelabrum tuum de loco moveat (Apoc. 2.5). Ædificaturus turrim, futuri operis sumptus supputa (Luc. 14.28). Infatuatum sal ad nihil est utile nisi ut projiciatur foras, et a porcis conculcetur. Monachus si ceciderit, rogabit pro eo Sacer-

that the heresy of the Nicolaites should arise from him as from its root (cf. Apoc. 2:6,15). Let each man examine himself, and thus draw near. Ecclesiastical rank DOES NOT MAKE a Christian. Cornelius the Centurion while still a pagan is cleansed by gift of the Holy Ghost (Acts 10). Daniel while still a boy judges the elders (Dan. 13): Amos, while picking blackberries from a bush, is suddenly turned into a prophet. David, a shepherd, is chosen to be king (1 King 16). It is the least disciple that Jesus loves most. Sit at the lower place, brother, that when your junior arrives, you may be ordered to move higher (Lk. 14). Upon whom will the Lord rest, if not on he who is humble and quiet, and trembles at His words (Is. 66:2)? More is demanded from him to whom much has been entrusted. *The mighty shall be mightily tormented (Wis. 6:7).* And let no man commend himself for mere bodily chastity, when men shall have to give answer in the day of judgement for every idle word they have uttered (Mt. 12:5), and even an insult towards a brother amounts to a crime of homicide. It is no easy thing to hold the place of Paul, to have the rank of Peter, both reigning now with Christ, unless, perchance, an angel come to tear the veil of your temple (Mt. 27:51), and move your candlestick

dos. Pro Sacerdotis lapsu quis rogaturus est ?

from its place (Apoc. 2:5). He who is about to build a tower computes well the cost of the work that awaits him (Lk. 14:28). Salt deprived of its taste is good for nothing but to be thrown out, to be trodden over by swine. If a Monk falls, the priest will pray for him. But for the fall of a Priest, who shall pray?

54 Letter 5 to Florentius, *In ea mihi parte*, 2; PL 22, 357: *Nosti hoc esse animæ Christianæ pabulum, si in lege Domini meditetur die ac nocte (Psal. 1).*

55 Letter 10 to Paul, *Humanæ vitæ brevitas*, 3; PL 22, 344: *Misimus interim te tibi, id est, Paulo seni Paulum seniorem…*

56 *Vita S. Pauli Primi Eremitæ*, 18; PL 23, 28: *Obsecro, quicumque hæc legis, ut Hieronymi peccatoris memineris: cui si Dominus optionem daret, multo magis eligeret tunicam Pauli cum meritis ejus, quam regum purpuras cum pœnis suis.*

57 See *Letter 22 to Eustochium, 7*; PL 22, 398-399.

O quoties ego ipse in eremo constitutus, et in illa vasta solitudine, quæ exusta solis ardoribus, horridum Monachis præstat habitaculum, putabam me Romanis interesse deliciis. Sedebam solus, quia amaritudine repletus eram. Horrebant sacco membra deformia, et squalida cutis situm æthiopicæ carnis obduxerat. Quotidie lacrymæ, quotidie gemitus, et si quando repugnantem somnus imminens oppressisset, nuda humo ossa vix hærentia collidebam. De cibis vero et potu taceo, cum etiam languentes Monachi aqua frigida utantur, et coctum aliquid accepisse, luxuria sit. Ille igitur ego, qui ob gehennæ metum, tali me carcere ipse damnaveram, scorpionum tantum socius et ferarum,

O how often, when established in my hermitage, and dwelling in that vast seclusion, which, ablaze with the sun's rays, provides a rugged place for monks to live, I thought myself to be amidst the pleasures which abound in Rome. I sat alone, for I was filled with bitterness; my unsightly members clothed in sackcloth shuddered, and scaly skin incased my sunburnt filthy flesh. Each day was filled with tears and groans, and when a looming sleepiness would overwhelm me, I, who battled sleep, would thump onto the earth the naked bones which scarcely clung to it. Concerning food and drink I do not speak, since even utterly infirm monks drink cold water, and to be given something cooked

sæpe choris intereram puellarum. Pallebant ora jejuniis, et mens desideriis æstuabat in frigido corpore, et ante hominem sua jam in carne præmortuum, sola libidinum incendia bulliebant. Itaque omni auxilio destitutus, ad Jesu jacebam pedes, rigabam lacrymis, crine tergebam ; et repugnantem carnem hebdomadarum inedia subjugabam. Non erubesco infelicitatis meæ miseriam confiteri, quin potius plango me non esse quod fuerim. Memini me clamantem, diem crebro junxisse cum nocte, nec prius a pectoribus cessasse verberibus, quam rediret, Domino increpante, tranquillitas. Ipsam quoque cellulam meam, quasi cogitationum mearum consciam pertimescebam. Et mihimet iratus et rigidus, solus deserta penetrabam. Sicubi concava vallium, aspera montium, rupium prærupta cernebam, ibi meæ orationis locus, ibi ilud miserrimæ carnis ergastulum ; et, ut ipse mihi testis est Dominus, post multas lacrymas, post cœlo inhærentes oculos, nonnunquam videbar mihi interesse agminibus Angelorum, et lætus gaudensque cantabam : *Post te in odorem unguentorum tuorum curremus (Cant. 1.3).*

is an extravagance. I, who so lived, therefore, and who, because of fear of hell, condemned myself to such a prison, and had for my companions only scorpions and beasts, would often find myself amidst a crowd of dancing girls. My face was pale from fasting, then in a frigid body, my mind in its concupiscence would burn, and nothing save the fires of desire would boil a man already dead before his actual death. Thus, bereft of all assistance, I'd lay prostrate at the feet of Jesus, to bathe them with my tears and dry them with my hair: and by my weekly fasts would conquer my rebellious flesh. I feel no shame to openly admit the misery of my unhappy state; I, on the contrary, regret that I am not now what then I was. I remember calling out non-stop from dawn to dusk, and would not cease inflincting bruises on my breast until tranquility, at the Lord's rebuke, would reappear. I feared my very cell, moreover, as if it were aware of all my thoughts, and both angry with myself and stern, I'd penetrate alone into the desert. If in any place I spotted caverns in the valleys, rough mountaintops, or jagged cliffs, there I'd make my place for prayer, there I'd drag the penitentiary of my poor flesh: and, calling on the Lord Himself to be my witness, after copious tears, after keeping my eyes fixed on heaven, I'd sometimes

see myself surrounded by Angelic hosts, and happily rejoicing would sing forth: *Close behind thee shall we run, amidst the fragrance of thy ointments (Cant. 1:3).*

58 See *Letter 22 to Eustochium, 30;* PL 22, 416-417.

Cum ante annos plurimos domo, parentibus, sorore, cognatis, et quid his difficilius est, consuetudinis lautioris cibi, propter cœlorum me regna castrassem, et Jerosolymam militaturus pergerem, Bibliotheca, quam mihi Romæ summo studio ac labore confeceram, carere omnino non poteram. Itaque miser ego lecturus Tullium, jejunabam. Post noctium crebras vigilias, post lacrymas, quas mihi præteritorum recordatio peccatorum ex imis visceribus eruebat, Plautus sumebatur in manus. Si quando in memetipsum reversus, Prophetas legere cœpissem, sermo horrebat incultus; et quia lumen cæcis oculis non videbam, non oculorum putabam culpam esse, sed solis. Dum ita me antiquus serpens illuderet, in media ferme Quadragesima medullis febris, corpus invasit exhaustum: et sine ulla requie (quod dictu quoque incredibile sit) sic infelicia membra depasta est, ut ossibus vix hærerem. Interim parantur exequiæ, et vitalis animæ calor, toto frigescente jam corpore, in solo tantum tepente pectusculo palpitabat: Cum subito raptus in spiritu, ad tribunal judi-

Many years ago, when, for the Kingdom of Heaven, I severed myself from parents, sister, relatives—and what was yet more difficult—my routine fare of finer foods, and journeyed towards Jerusalem to offer service in Christ's army, I simply could not do without the library which I had copied out with utmost care and toil during my student days in Rome. Thus I, a wretch, would fast, and afterwards read Cicero. After repeated all-night vigils, after the tears which memory of my former sins would draw out of my deepest core, I'd take up Plautus in my hands. If every now and then I'd come back to myself and start to read the Prophets, their unpolished discourse made me shudder, and since I could not see the light with my blind eyes, I thought this was the sun's fault, not my eyes'. While the ancient serpent thus made sport of me, about mid-Lent, a marrow-piercing fever invaded my exhausted body, and utterly deprived of rest, my miserable limbs were so consumed, that—something unbelievable to say—they scarcely clung unto my bones. In

cis pertrahor; ubi tantum luminis, et tantum erat ex circumstantium claritate fulgoris, ut projectus in terram, sursum aspicere non auderem. Interrogatus de conditione, Christianum me esse respondi. Et ille qui præsidebat : Mentiris, ait, Ciceronianus es, non Christianus : ubi enim thesaurus tuus, ibi et cor tuum (Matth. 6.21). Illico obmutui, et inter verbera (nam cædi me jusserat) conscientiæ magis igne torquebar, illum mecum versiculum reputans : «In inferno autem quis confitebitur tibi» (Ps. 6.6) ? Clamare tamen cœpi, et ejulans dicere : Miserere mei, Domine, miserere mei. Hæc vox inter flagella resonabat. Tandem ad præsidentis genua provoluti qui astabant, precabantur, ut veniam tribueret adolescentiæ, et errori locum pœnitentiæ commodaret, exacturus deinde cruciatum, si Gentilium litterarum libros aliquando legissem. Ego qui in tanto constrictus articulo, vellem etiam majora promittere, dejetare cœpi, et nomen ejus obtestans, dicere, Domine si unquam habuero codices sæculares, si legero, te negavi. In hæc sacramenti verba dimissus, revertor ad superos; et mirantibus cunctis, oculos aperto tanto lacrymarum imbre perfusos, ut etiam, incredulis fidem facerem ex dolore. Nec vero sopor ille fuerat, aut vana somnia, quibus sæpe deludimur. Testis est tribual illud, ante quod jacui, testis judicium tri-

the meantime, the funeral was being planned, and as all of my body was now growing cold, the spirit's vital warmth would only pulsate in my tepid heart alone. When, suddenly, snatched up in spirit, I am hauled to the tribunal of the judge, where such brightness, such dazzling splendor radiated from those standing round, that, prostrate on the ground, I dared not raise my sight. When asked about what teaching I adopted in my life, I answered that I was a Christian. Then he who at the court presided said: You lie! You are no Christian, but a Ciceronian, for where your treasure is, there also is your heart (Mt. 6:21). There and then I found myself bereft of speech, and amidst the thrashings (for he charged me to be whipped), I suffered at the pangs of conscience all the more, turning over in myself that verse: "In hell, however, who shall praise Thee?" (Ps. 6:6). I started to cry out, and wailing said: "Have mercy on me, Lord, have mercy," the sound of which resounded through the beatings. At length, those gathered round fell prostrate at the judge's knees, beseeching him grant clemency to youthful age, and accord a place of penance to my erring custom, but promise to inflict grim torments, should I again read pagan authors. Trapped as I was in such a dreadful moment, I longed to promise

ste, quod timui : ita mihi nunquam contingat in talem incidere quæstionem. Liventes fateor habuisse me scapulas, plagas sensisse post somnum, et tanto dehinc studio divina legisse, quanto non ante mortalia legeram.

greater things, and began to swear in solemn fashion; and appealing to His name declared, "Lord if ever I read worldly books again, I have denied Thee." Released amidst these phrases of my sacred oath, I come back to this world; and with all watching in amazement, I open eyes suffused with such a flood of tears, that from my woe I'd kindle faith even in skeptics. And truly that was neither stupor, nor a chain of empty dreams, by which we often are deceived. That tribunal, before which I lay prostrate, is my witness, as is the doleful judgment which I feared. May it never come to pass that I should meet with such a questioning again. I confess that I had shoulders bruised and sore, and that once the dream had passed still felt the wounds. Thenceforth I read the sacred tomes with so much zeal, as never I had done with mortal books.

59 Cf. *Commentary on Galatians*, Book 3, Chap. 5; PL 26, 399: *Nostis enim et ipsæ, quod plus quam quindecim anni sunt, ex quo in manus meas numquam Tullius, numquam Maro, numquam gentilium litterarum quilibet Auctor ascendit: et si quid forte inde dum loquimur, obrepit, quasi antique per nebulam somnii recordamur.*
Also, *Adversus Rufinus*. Lib. 1, 30; PL 23, 421-422, where Jerome describes his infancy, and how the learning of pagan literature was mercilessly drilled into him. *Dixi me sæculares litteras deinceps non lecturum: de futuro sponsio est, non præteritæ memoriæ abolitio. Et quomodo, inquires, tenes, quod tanto tempore non relegis? Rursum si aliquid de veteribus libris respondero, et dixero,* adeo in teneris consuescere multum est (Virgil, Gerog. II): *dum renuo, crimen incurro, et pro me testimonium proferens, hoc ipso arguor, quo defendor.*

Scilicet nunc longo sermone texendum est, quod probant conscientiæ singulorum. Quis nostrum non meminit infantiæ suæ ?... Et quo magis stupeas, nunc cano et recalvo capite, sæpe mihi videor in somnis comatulus, et sumpta toga, ante rhetorem controversiolam declamare. Cumque experrectus fuero, gratulor me dicendi periculo liberatum. Crede mihi, multa ad purum recordatur infantia. Si litteras didicisses, oleret testa ingenioli tui, quo semel fuisset imbuta.
He uses the same analogy of the bottle keeping its original scent in Letter 10 to Paul of Concordia, *Humanæ vitæ brevitas*, 3; PL 22, 344: *Sed nescio quomodo, etiam si aqua plena sit, tamen eumdem odorem lagena servat, quo dum rudis esset, imbuta est.*

60 Cf. Preface to his translation of the *Chronicon* of Eusebius Phamphillius; PL 27, 36: *Inde adeo venit, ut sacræ litteræ minus comptæ, et dure sonantes videantur, quod diserti homines interpretatas eas de Hebræo nescientes, dum superficiem, non medullam inspiciunt, ante quasi vestem orationis sordidam perhorrescant, quam pulchrum intrinsecus rerum corpus inveniant. Denique quid Psalterio canorius? quod in morem nostri Flacci, et Græci Pindari, nunc iambo currit, nunc alcaico personat, nunc Sapphico tumet, nunc semipede ingreditur. Quid Deuteronomii et Isaiæ Cantico pulchrius? quid Salomone gravius? quid perfectius Job? Quæ omnia hexametris et pentametris versibus, ut Josephus et Origenes scribunt, apud suos composita decurrunt. Hæc cum Græca legimus, aliud quiddam sonant; cum Latine, penitus non cohærent.*

61 See *Letter 125, to the Monk Rusticus*, 12; PL 22, 1079.

Dum essem juvenis, et solitudinis me deserta vallarent, incentiva vitiorum ardoremque naturæ ferre non poteram, quem cum crebris jejuniis frangerem, mens tamen cogitationibus æstuabat. Ad quam edomandam, cuidam fratri, qui ex Hebræis crediderat, me in disciplinam dedi, ut post Quntiliani acumina, Ciceronis fluvios, gravitatemque Frontonis, et lenitatem Plinii, alphabetum discerem, et stridentia anhelantiaque verba me-

When I was young, and the solitude of the desert walled me in on all sides, I could not endure the allurments of vice and the vehemence of nature, which, though I would quash with frequent fasts, my mind, nonetheless, would still boil with troubling thoughts. In order to tame it, thus, I consigned myself to a certain brother who, from the Jews, came to the faith, so that, after the subtlety of Quintilian, the fluent speeches of Cicero,

ditarer. Quid ibi laboris insumpserim, quid sustinuerim difficultatis, quoties desperaverim, quotiesque cessaverim, et contentione discendi rursus incœperim, testis est conscientia, tam mea qui passus sum, quam eorum qui mecum duxerunt vitam. Et gratias ago Domino, quod de amaro semine litterarum, dulces fructus carpo.

the solemn dignity of Fronto, and the smoothness of Pliny, I should learn anew my letters, and drill myself with words of aspirated harshness. My conscience, and that of they who shared my life then are the witnesses of the great toil that it cost me, of what difficulty I endured, how often I despaired, how often I gave up, then once again, thanks to an eager striving after learning, would start anew. And I thank the Lord that from the bitter seed of study, I now reap luscious fruits.

CHAPTER 4: THE ANTIOCHIAN SCHISM AND THE END OF HIS DESERT EXPERIENCE

62 See *Letter 17 to Mark the Priest*, 3; PL 22, 360.

Non mihi conceditur unus angulus eremi. Quotidie exposcor fidem, quasi sine fide renatus sim. Confiteor, ut volunt, non placet. Unum tantum placet, ut hinc recedam. Jamjam cedo : abruperunt a me partem animæ meæ, carissimos fratres: ecce discedere cupiunt, imo discedunt, Melius esse dicentes, inter feras habitare, quam cum talibus Christianis.

Not one corner of this desert is granted me. Every day my faith is questioned, as if I were reborn deprived of it each day. I make a confession, as they desire, but it fails to satisfy. One thing alone satisfies them, that I leave this place. I now yield, for they tore away from me part of my soul, my dearest brothers. See, they want to leave me, indeed, they are leaving, saying that "it is better to live with the beasts than with Christians like you."

63 Cf. Letter 15, 1; PL 22, 355: *Neque vero tanta vastitas elementi liquentis, et interjacens longitudo terrarum, me a pretiosæ margaritæ potuit inquisitione prohibere.*

64 Ibid. *Profligato a sobole mala patrimonio, apud vos solos incorrupta patrum servatur hæreditas.*

65 Ibid. *Quicumque tecum non colligit, spargit : hoc est, qui Christi non est, Antichristi est.* See also Letter 16, 2; PL 22, 359: *Ego interim clamito, si quis cathedræ Petri jungitur, meus est. Meletius, Vitalis, atque Paulinus tibi hærere se dicunt, possem credere si hoc unus assereret. Nunc aut duo mentiuntur, aut omnes.*

66 Vitalis, though once orthodox, became a follower of Apollinaris of Laodicea; nevertheless, he deceitfully tried to *seem* orthodox and to this end was duplicitous in his speech. Jerome, unaware of this, listed him among the orthodox claimants whereas in fact there were only two orthodox claimants—Meletius and Paulinus.

67 *Historia Ecclesiastica,* Lib. II, Cap. XLIV; PG 67, 355-358.

68 Jerome would tell us many years later (398) that Eusthatius was the first bishop of Antioch to openly sound the trumpet of war against the Arians, cf. Letter 73 to Evangelum, 2; PG 22, 677: *Eustathium nostrum, qui primus Antiochenæ Ecclesiæ Episcopus contra Arium clarissima tuba bellicum cecinit.*

69 Cf. Socrates, *Historia Ecclesiastica,* Lib. III. Cap. IX; PG 67, 403-406.

70 Cf. Cf. Socrates, *Historia Ecclesiastica,* Lib. III. Cap. V-VI: PG 67, 387-390; also Lib. III. Cap. IX; PG 67, 403-406.

71 Cf. Sozomen, *Historia Ecclesiastica,* Lib. III, Cap. XX; PG 67, 1099: *Verum Athanasius…cum iis vero qui Eustathiani vocabantur, communionem iniit, in privatis ædibus collectas celebrans; Ἀθανάσιος τοῖς καλουμένοις Εὐσταθιανοῖς ἐκοινώνει, ἐν ἰδιωτῶν οἰκίαις ἐκκλησιάζων.* Here Sozomen relates that Paulinus' group, the followers of Eustathius, offered the Liturgy in private homes, perhaps at a time when they were deprived of a Church of their own, or when their numbers exceeded the capacity of the small church granted to Paulinus by Euzoius. The Greek original is quite vivid: *Athanasius would communicate with those called Eustathians, "churching" in private homes.*

72 Cf. PG 26, 795-810.

73 Lucifer was not in full agreement with the proceedings of the Alexandrian Synod, in particular their decision to re-admit bishops who, though orthodox, had collaborated in minor, and comprehensible, ways with the Arians, such as Meletius. He thus gave rise to a group of followers who refused to commune with such prelates. Jerome once witnessed a dispute between a Lucife-

rian and an orthodox believer in Antioch that was so intense that it needed to be prolonged for several days. This dispute formed the basis for the famous *Dialogue Against the Luciferians* which Jerome wrote near the time of his priestly ordination, and in which he refuted their errors. The Luciferians gave the impression that only the island of Sardinia, home of Lucifer's episcopal see, would be saved. The orthodox interlocuter thus exclaims: "If Christ has no Church, or if in Sardinia alone He has one, He has become exceedingly poor" *(Si Ecclesiam non habet Christus, aut si in Sardinia tantum habet, nimium pauper factus est)*. The Dialogue is invaluable for the account of early Church history it provides, in particular, of the deceptive council of Rimini, in which a host of orthodox bishops were tricked into consenting to a semi-Arian creed. In that context Jerome wrote his famous line: "The whole world groaned, and was astonished to see itself Arian" *(Ingemuit totus orbis, et Arianum se esse miratus est)*. But God provided for his Church when, at the rise of a new emperor, the Arian hegemony ceased and orthodox bishops were allowed to return to their sees: "Then Egypt received its conquering Athanasius: then the Church of Gaul embraced Hilary, returning from battle; then upon Eusebius (of Vercelli's) return Italy exchanged its mourning garb" (*Tunc triumphatorem suum Athanasium Ægyptus excepit: tunc Hilarium de prælio revertentem, Galliarum Ecclesia complexa est; tunc ad reditum Eusebii lugubres vestes Italia mutavit*). Then the poor bishops who had been tricked into signing the impious creed repented of their slight fault; and, it is asked, how could one not receive them back? See PL 23, 168-169 and 172-173.

74 Cf. Letter 15, 1; PL 22, 357: *Tota sæcularium litterarum schola nihil aliud* hypostasim, *nisi usian novit.*

75 The Alexandrian took place a good decade before St. Basil worked out the orthodox understanding of the term *hypóstasis* (373-375, the years in which *De Spiritu Sancto* was written), and nearly two decades before the Church finally settled the question at the Council of Constantinople (381).

CHAPTER 5: PRIESTLY ORDINATION AND STUDIES IN ANTIOCH AND CONSTANTINOPLE, 380-382

76 Cf. Socrates, V, XV; PG 67, 601-602, footnote variorum z indicates this happened in 389. But this footnote confuses Evagrius of *Antioch* with Evagrius *Ponticus* by directing you to Soc. IV. 23 . . . one must have caution with various important personages sharing the same name!

77 That Damasus was in communion with Paulinus is demonstrated by a letter he wrote to Paulinus *as bishop of Antioch* advising him how he should receive those withdrawing from communion with Vitalis, cf. *Letter of Damasus Pope of Rome to Paulinus Bishop of the City of Antioch*, PL 13, col. 354-364. This letter should not be taken to mean, however, that Damasus rejected communion with Meletius; he seems to have been open to communion with both bishops as both were reputed to be orthodox. It makes sense, however, that he should have addressed *Paulinus* with the question of ex-followers of Vitalis because Vitalis had formerly been one of Meletius' priests, but had separated himself from him due to a falling out with his co-presbyter at the time, Flavian, who at the time closely assisted Meletius and later succeeded him as bishop, and thereupon sided with Apollinaris of Laodicea (the history of which is related in Sozomen, VI, 25). Damasus, solicitous for the salvation of those souls, turned to Paulinus as the only orthodox bishop who could help the situation.

78 In his massive work *Adversus Hæreses,* also known as the *Panarium* or "little ark" (Lib. III, Tom. II, XX-XXI, PG 42, col. 671-674) Epiphanius relates how he first met Paulinus on a visit to Antioch when he and Vitalis (the bishop of the sect of Apollinaris) were in heated debate with each other; Paulinus, in order to prove his orthodoxy, showed Epiphanius the confession of faith he made at the request of St. Athanasius and the Alexandrian synod of 362. He thenceforward enjoyed Epiphanius' support, whereas Vitalis was discovered by the shrewd old bishop to be a disciple of Apollinaris masquerading as a Catholic.

79 His memorial is kept by the Roman Martyrology on May 12: *At Salamina in Cyprus, St Epiphanius, Bishop, who excelled in manifold learning and the knowledge of sacred letters, and stood forth remark-*

able for holiness of life, zeal for the Catholic faith, generosity towards the poor, and the power of miracles.

80 See the introduction given to the three volumes containing Epiphanius's works in PG 41, on the first page after the table of contents.

81 *The Sayings of the Desert Fathers*, Trans. Benedicta Ward, SLG Cistercian Publications, 1975, p. 58

82 See the opening lines of his *Commentary on Isaiah*; PL 24, 18:

Expletis longo vix tempore in duodecim Prophetas viginti explanationum libris, et in Danielem Commentariis, cogis me, virgo Christi Eustochium, transire ad Isaiam: et quod sanctæ matri tuæ Paulæ, dum viveret, pollicitus sum, tibi reddere. Quod quidem et eruditissimo viro fratri tuo Pammachio promisisse me memini; cumque in affectu par sis, vincis præsentia. Itaque et tibi et illi per te reddo quod debeo, obediens Christi præceptis, qui ait : *Scrutamini Scripturas (Joan. V, 39)* ; et, *Quærite, et invenietis (Matth. VII,76)*. Ne illud audiam cum Judæis : *Erratis, nescientes Scripturas, neque virtutem Dei (Matth. XXII,29)*. Si enim juxta apostolum Paulum (II Cor. I, 24) Christus Dei virtus est, Deique sapientia ; et qui nescit Scripturas, nescit Dei virtutem ejusque sapientiam : ignoratio Scripturarum, ignoratio Christi est.

Having just expended much time in compiling the 20 books of exegesis on the 12 Minor Prophets and the Prophet Daniel, now you compel me, virgin of Christ, Eusthochium, to move on to Isaiah: and to pay to you that which I promised to give to your holy mother, Paula, while she lived. I remember, furthermore, to have made the same promise to Pammachius, your brother (i.e. brother-in-law as he was married to her sister Paulina). And though you are equal to them in my affection, nevertheless you take the prize, as you are here present. Therefore, I will pay the debt that I owe to them as well as to you through you, obedient to the precept of Christ, who said: *Search the Scriptures (Jn. 5:39)*; and, *Seek and you shall find (Mt. 7:76)*, lest I should hear along with the Jews: *You err because you know neither the Scriptures nor the power of God (Mt. 22:29)*. If, indeed, according to the apostle Paul (2 Cor. 1:24) Christ is the power of God and the wisdom of God; and he who is ignorant of the Scriptures is ignorant of the power and the wisdom of God, then ignorance of the Scriptures is ignorance of Christ.

83 The only anecdote connected to St. Basil preserved in the *Apophthegmata Patrum* illustrates this attitude: *One of the old men said, 'When Saint Basil came to the monastery one day, he said to the abbot, after the customary exhortation, "Have you a brother here who is obedient?" The other replied, "They are all your servants, master, and strive for their salvation." But he replied, "Have you a brother who is really obedient?" Then the abbot led a brother to him and Saint Basil used him to serve during the meal. When the meal was ended, the brother brought him some water for rinsing his hands and Saint Basil said to him, "Come here, so that I also may offer you water." The brother allowed the bishop to pour the water. Then Saint Basil said to him, "When I enter the sanctuary, come, that I may ordain you deacon." When this was done, he ordained him priest and took him with him to the bishop's palace because of his obedience.'* Cf. *The Sayings of the Desert Fathers,* Trans. Benedicta Ward, SLG Cistercian Publications, 1975, pp. 39-40.

84 Cf. *De Cœnobiorum Instit. Lib. XII, Caput XVII* ; PL 49, 418. In his chapter on vainglory Cassian—himself both monk and priest—stresses how the clerical state makes it more difficult for the monk to overcome this vice:

Quapropter hæc est antiquitus Patrum permanens nunc usque sententia, quam proferre sine mea confusione non potero, qui nec germanam vitare potui, nec episcopi evadere manus, omnimodis monachum fugere debere mulieres et episcopos. Neuter enim sinit eum, quem semel suæ familiaritati devinxerit, vel quieti cellulæ ulterius operam dare, vel divinæ theoriæ per sanctarum rerum intuitum purissimis oculis inhærere.

For which reason, this is the time-honored opinion held by the Fathers even now (which I relate to my own shame, for I was not able to avoid seeing my sister, or evade the hands of a bishop): that a monk should at all costs steer clear of women and bishops. Neither of these, indeed, permit the man who even once has been overcome by their acquaintance to give himself up to the work of a quiet cell, or to cling to divine contemplation through the perception of holy things with wholly untainted eyes.

85 See *Against John of Jerusalem*, 41; PL 23, 395.

A me misello homine sanctæ memoriæ episcopus Paulinus audivit : "Num rogavi te, ut ordinarer ? Si sic presbyterium tribuis, ut monachum nobis non auferas, tu videris de judicio tuo. Sin autem sub nomine presbyteri tollis mihi, propter quod sæculum dereliqui : ego habeo quod semper habui : nullum dispendium in ordinatione passus es."

The bishop Paulinus of blessed memory heard from me, a wretch of a man: "Did I ask you to be ordained? If in conferring the priesthood you do not deprive us of the monastic state, do as it seems best to you. But if by the title of priest you divest me of that on account of which I forsook the world, I hold on to that which I've always had: you have suffered no loss in this ordination."

86 See the *Commentary on Jeremiah*, Introduction to Book 3; PL 24, 757-758:

Hoc ego cum facere cuperem... Scripturarum sanctarum explanationi insistere, et hominibus linguæ meæ, Hebræorum, Græcorumque eruditionem trader...

As the object I wished to pursue is... to intently pursue the expounding of Holy Scripture, and to hand on to those of my native language the erudition of Hebrews and Greeks...

87 Cf. *Letter 84 to Pammachius and Oceanus*; PL 22, 745.

88 Cf. *Letter 50 to Domnionem*, PL 22, 513; *Commentary on Isaiah*, Book 3, Chap. 6, PL. 24, 91.

89 Cf. *Letter 84 to Pammachius and Oceanus*, PL 22, 749-750: *Quis nostrum tanta potest legere, quanta ille conscripsit? Quis ardentem in Scripturis animum non miretur?*

90 See Georges Florovsky's *Christianity and Culture: Volume Two*, Nordland Publishing Company, 1974, p. 101. See also p. 109-110: *Should we not explain the obvious popularity of the Iconoclastic bias among the learned bishops and clergy...on the basis of their Origenistic learning?...The Orient especially was infected by Origenistic ideas of all sorts...the whole tenor and ethos of Origenism was undoubtedly favorable to that course of theological reasoning which was actually adopted by the Iconoclasts. Therefore, the defense of Holy Icons was, in some sense, an indirect refutation of Origenism, a new act in the story of the "Origenistic controversies."*

[91] See *Letter 18 to Damasus*, 4; PL 22, 363.

Quidam ante me tam Græci quam Latini hunc locum exponentes, Dominum super thronum sedentem, Deum Patrem; et duo Seraphim, quæ ex utraque parte stantia prædicantur, Dominum nostrum Jesum Christum, et Spiritum Sanctum interpretati sunt. Quorum ego auctoritati, quamvis sint eruditissimi, non assentior. MULTO SIQUIDEM MELIUS EST vera rustice, quam falsa diserte proferre: maxime cum Johannes Evangelista in hac eadem Visione, non Deum Patrem, sed Christum scribat esse conspectum. Nam cum de incredulitate diceret Judæorum, statim causas incredulitatis exposuit, dicens: *Et ideo non poterant credere in eum, quia dixit Isaias: Aure audietis, et non intelligetis: et cernentes aspicietis, et non videbitis. Hæc autem dixit, quando vidit gloriam Unigeniti, et testificatus est de eo (Is. 6.9.19 ; Joan. 12.40.41).* In præsenti egro volumine Isaiæ ab eo qui sedet in throno jubetur, ut dicat: *Aure audietis, et non intelligetis.* Qui autem hæc jubet, ut Evangelista intelligit, Christus est : unde nunc colligitur, non posse Seraphim Christum intelligi, cum Christus sit ipse qui sedeat.

Certain persons before me, both Greek and Latin, expounding this passage have reckoned the Lord sitting upon the throne to be God the Father, and the two Seraphim that stand on either side crying out to be our Lord Jesus Christ and the Holy Ghost. Though they be among the most erudite authorities, I do not assent to their interpretation. IT IS MUCH BETTER to say true things in modest and unadorned speech, than to pronounce false things with great eloquence; this is especially the case in this passage, since in this very Vision, John the Evangelist said it was Christ who was seen, not God the Father. Indeed, when speaking of the unbelief of the Jews he said: *And therefore they could not believe, because Isaias said again: He hath blinded their eyes and hardened their heart, that they should not see with their eyes, nor understand with their heart and be converted: and I should heal them. These things said Isaias, when he saw his glory and spoke of him (Is. 6:9,19; Jn 12:40-41).* In the present volume of Isaiah, therefore, it is commanded by Him who sits on the throne to say: *Hearing, hear and understand not.* But He who commands these things, as the Evangelist understands, is Christ: from this it can now be gathered that the Seraphim cannot be Christ, if it is Christ Himself who is seated.

92 Ibid.

Quidquid enim in veteri legimus Testamento, hoc idem in Evangelio reperimus: et quod in Evangelio fuerit lectitatum, hoc ex veteris Testamenti auctoritate deducitur: nihil in eis dissonum, nihil diversum est. *Et dicebant, Sanctus, Sanctus, Sanctus Dominus Deus Sabaoth.* In ambobus Testamentis Trinitas prædicatur.

That which we read in the Old Testament we likewise find in the New: and what is read in the Gospel can be concluded by the authority of the Old Testament; nothing in them is dissonant, nothing is dissimilar. *And they cried out, Holy, Holy, Holy Lord God of Hosts.* In both Testaments the Trinity is proclaimed.

CHAPTER 6: JEROME'S SECOND PERIOD IN ROME, 382-385

93 Many years later, Jerome would refer to having been solicited or induced to go to Rome by compelling church matters, *Ecclesiastica traxisset necessitas.* It is not clear, though, whether he was persuaded on his own by the gravity of the matter, or sought out by Damasus, or Paulinus or Epiphanius, or all of the above. See Letter 127 to Principia, PL 22, 1091.

94 Cf. *Letter 108 to Eustochium,* 6; PL 22, 881: *Cumque Orientis et Occidentis episcopos ob quasdam ecclesiarum dissensions Romam imperiales litteræ contraxissent...*

95 See *Letter 123 to Ageruchiam,* 10; PL 22, 1052: *Ante annos plurimos, cum in chartis Ecclesiasticis juvarem Damasum Romanæ urbis Episcopum, et Orientis atque Occidentis Synodicis consultationibus responderem...*

96 *Letter 45 to Asella,* 3; PL 22, 481.

97 *Preface to the Four Gospels to Damasus*; PL 29, 525-528.

Novum opus facere me cogis ex veteri, ut post exemplaria Scripturarum toto orbe dispersa, quasi quidam arbiter sedeam: et quia inter se variant, quæ sint illa quæ cum Græca consentient veritate, decernam. Pius labor, sed periculosa præsumptio, judicare de

You urge me to prepare a new work out of one long in existence, and to preside as judge over the copies of the Scriptures which have been dispersed in all the world; and since these disagree among themselves, to judge which ones conform to the authentic Greek

cæteris, ipsum ab ómnibus judicandum: senis mutare linguam, et canescentem jam mundum ad initia retrahere parvulorum. Quis enim doctus partier vel indoctus, cum in manus volume assumpserit, et a saliva, quam semel imbibit, viderit discrepare quod lectitat, non statim erumpat in vocem, me falsarium, me clamans esse sacrilegum, qui audeam aliquid in veteribus libris addere, mutare, corrigere? Adversus quam invidiam duplex causa me consolatur: quod et tu, qui summus Sacerdos es, fieri jubes: et verum non esse quod variat, etiam maledicorum testimonio comprobatur. Se enim Latinis exemplaribus fides est adhibenda, respondeant, quibus: tot enim sunt exemplaria pene quot codices. Sin autem veritas est quærenda de pluribus : cur non ad Græcam originem revertentes, ea quæ vel a vitiosis interpretibus male edita, vel a præsumptoribus imperitis emendata perversius, vel a librariis dormitantibus addita sunt, aut mutata, corrigimus ? ... Igitur hæc præsens præfatiuncula pollicetur quatuor tantum Evangelia, quorum ordo est iste, Matthæus, Marcus, Lucas, Joannes, codicum Græcorum emendata collatione, sed Veterum. Quæ ne multum a lectionis Latinæ consuetudine discreparent, ita calamo temperavimus, ut his tantum quæ sensum videbantur mutare, correctis, reli-

originals. It is a pious undertaking, though, too, a risky boldness, to sit in judgment with respect to others, while I myself am to be judged by all: to change the language of one advanced in years, and bring a gray-haired world back to the early stages of mere children. Who, truly, be he learned or untaught, when taking up into his hands a scroll which, reading with attention, he discerns to differ from the flavor which he once imbibed, will not swiftly erupt into an outcry, shouting out that I'm a sacrilegious forger for daring to add something to the ancient books, or alter or correct them? Two things console me in the face of such ill-will: that you, who are the high Priest, order it be done: and that those volumes which conflict among themselves cannot all likewise be authentic, something which is demonstrated even by the claims of my detractors. Indeed, if credibility is to be given to the Latin manuscripts, let them tell us, to which ones? There are virtually as many versions as there are copies. But if a true text is to be sought among these many versions, why do we not, returning to the source in Greek, correct those things which had been badly published by deficient translators, or "corrected" for the worse, by those who were audacious and incompetent, or added to or changed by sleeping copyists? ...

qua manere pateremur ut fuerant. Canones quoque, quos Eusebius Cæsariensis episcopus Alexandrinum secutus Ammonium, in decem numeros ordinavit, sicut in Græco habentur, expressimus. Quod si quis de curiosis voluerit nosse, quæ in Evangeliis, vel eadem, vel vicina, vel sola sint, eorum distinctione cognoscat. Magnus siquidem hic in nostris codicibus error inolevit, dum quod in eadem re alius Evangelista plus dixit, in alio quia minus putaverint, addiderunt. Vel dum eumdem sensum alius aliter expressit, ille qui unum e quatuor primum legerat, ad ejus exemplum cæteros quoque æstimaverit emendandos. Unde accidit, ut apud nox mixta sint omnia, et in Marco plura Lucæ atque Matthæi: rursum in Mattheo plura Joannis et Marci, et in cæteris reliquorum quæ aliis propria sunt, inveniantur. Cum itaque Canones legeris, qui subjecti sunt, confusionis errore sublato, et similia omnium scies, et singulis sua quæque restitues.

Therefore, this little preface simply promises four Gospels—of which this is the order: Matthew, Mark, Luke, and John—revised through a comparison with the ancient Greek originals. And lest they differ much from the established custom of the Latin reading, we have so restrained our quill, that those things only have been rectified which patently misconstrued the sense, and have suffered all the rest to stay unaltered. We have included, furthermore, the ten-fold rules, which Eusebius of Caesarea, following the example of Ammonius of Alexandria, devised. Wherefore if someone wishes to inquire about those things which are the same, or similar or unique, in all the Gospels, he may understand these matters through the divisions they establish. For, indeed, a serious mistake has lodged itself into our volumes, in that, where one Evangelist said more about a certain point, his content was included in the record of another, since such a narrative was held to be deficient. Or where the same meaning was conveyed with different words by the Evangelists, the rendering first encountered by the copyist was applied to all the others. And so, it happens as at night when all things get confused, and in Mark's text there is more of Luke and Matthew; or again, in Matthew there is more of John and Mark, and in them all are found things proper to the others. Therefore, when you read over these rules which are included, and the perplexities of error have been displaced, you will know which things are held in common, and will restore to each that which belongs to him alone.

98 The Roman Martyrology commemorates her feastday on January 31.

99 Cf. *Letter 127 to Principia*, PL 22, 1090.

100 It was to Vincent, and a certain Gallienus, that Jerome, while still in Constantinople, dedicated one of his earliest and most ambitious works, his translation of Eusebius of Cæsarea's Historical Chronicle, which documented the important moments of history in all the great civilizations of the Middle Eastern and Mediterranean world. Jerome enriched the original with his own detailed knowledge of Roman history, and updated the work up to his own day. Prosper of Aquitaine subsequently updated it even further, indicating the day of St. Jerome's passing and other important moments in the life of the great doctor. See PL 27,34.

101 Vincent, Eusebius and Paulinian would all follow Jerome to Bethlehem and live the monastic life there with him.

102 Cf. *Letter 45 to Asella*, PL 22, 482: *Ego faba ventrem impleo.* Also *Letter 22 to Eustochium*, 35 (PL 22, 420), where the fasting and abstinence customs of cenobitic monasteries, probably of Pachomian inspiration, are described. The way of life he established in the desert must have been similar to this, if not more austere: *Post horam nonam in commune concurritur, Psalmi resonant, Scripturæ recitantur ex more. Et completis orationibus, cunctisque residentibus, medius, quem Patrem vocant, incipit disputare...Post hæc concilium solvitur, et unaquaque decuria cum suo parente pergit ad mensas, quibus per singulas hebdomadas vicissim ministrant. Nullus in cibo strepitus est; nemo comedens loquitur. Vivitur pane, leguminibus et oleribus, quæ sale solo condiuntur...Jejunium totius anni æquale est, excepta Quadragesima, in qua sola conceditur districtius vivere. A Pentecoste cœnæ mutantur in prandia: quo et traditioni Ecclesiasticæ satisfiat, et ventrem cibo non onerent duplicato.*

103 Cf. Letter 22 to Eustochium, 37 (PL 22, 421), where he describes the canonical hours, which did not yet include Prime or Compline: *Post hæc quanquam Apostolus orare nos semper jubeat, ET SANCTIS etiam ipse sit somnus oratio, sic tamen divisas orandi horas debemus habere, ut si forte aliquo fuerimus opere detenti, ipsum nos ad officium tempus admoneat. Horam tertiam, sextam, nonam, diluculum quoque et vesperam, nemo est qui nesciat. Nec cibi sumantur, nisi oratione præmissa: nec recedatur a mensa, nisi referatur Creatori gratia. Noctibus bis terque surgendum, revolvenda quæ de Scripturis memoriter retinemus.* St. Benedict would later gather these segments, which the liturgical tradition would refer to as "nocturns", into one nocturnal prayer vigil.

104 We can be sure Jerome practiced the customs he advised to Eustochium (Letter 22, PL 22, 404): *Rarus sit egressus in publicum . . . Crebrius lege, disce quamplurima.*

105 See *Letter 24 to Marcella,* PL 22, 427-428. Her memorial is kept by the Roman Martyrology on December 6.

106 Her memorial is kept by the Roman Martyrology on January 26.

107 Her memorial is kept by the Roman Martyrology on September 28.

108 See *Letter 45 to Asella,* 3; PL 22, 481.

Nulla fuit alia Romæ matronarum, quæ meam posset edomare mentem, nisi lugens atque jejunans, squalens sordibus, fletibus pene cæcata; quam continuis noctibus misericordiam Domini deprecantem sol sæpe deprehendit. Cujus Canticum Psalmi, sermo Evangelium, deliciæ continentia, vita jejunium. Nulla me potuit alia delectare, nisi illa, quam manducantem nunquam vidi.

There was in Rome no other noblewoman who could so capture my mind, save she who always mourned and fasted, who, shabby and unkempt, was nearly rendered blind from many tears, and who would watch entire nights beseeching God for mercy till the sun would often find her still awake. She, whose songs of choice were Psalms, whose talk the Gospel, whose pleasure continence and life itself a fast. No woman could bring me so much delight, save her whom never I beheld partake of food.

109 Cf. *Letter 108 to Eustochium*, 6; PL 22, 881: *Cumque Orientis et Occidentis episcopos ob quasdam ecclesiarum dissensiones Romam imperiales litteræ contraxissent, vidit admirabiles viros, Christique pontifices, Paulinum Antiochenæ urbis episcopum, et Epiphanium Salaminæ Cypri, quæ nunc Constantia dicitur; quorum Epiphanium etiam hospitem habuit: Paulinum in aliena manentem domo, quasi proprium, humanitate possedit. Quorum accensa virtutibus, per momenta patriam deserere cogitabat.*

110 Cf. *Letter 127 to Principia*, 7; PL 22, 1091: *Denique cum et me Romam cum sanctis Pontificibus, Paulino et Epiphanio, Ecclesiastica traxisset necessitas…et verecunde nobilium feminarum oculos declinarem, ita egit secundum Apostolum,* importune, opportune (2. Tim. 4), *ut pudorem meum sua superaret industria. Et quia alicujus tunc nominis esse existimabar super studio Scripturarum, nunquam convenit, quin de Scripturis aliquid interrogaret : nec ut statim acquiesceret, sed moveret e contrario quæstiones ; non ut contenderet, sed ut quærendo disceret earum solutiones, quas opponi posse intelligebat.*

111 See *Letter XXIV to Marcella*, 1; PL 22, 427, where he praises the way of life of the virgin Asella after having praised Lea, a widow who occupied the second place in the order of chastity: *Nudiustertius de beatæ memoriæ Lea aliqua dixeramus : illico pupugit animum, et mihi venit in mentem, non debere nos tacere de Virgine, qui de secundo ordine castitatis locuti sumus.*

112 *Letter XXII to Eustochium*, 38; PL 22, 422: *Propone tibi beatam Mariam, quæ tantæ exstitit puritatis, ut Mater Domini esse mereretur.*

113 Cf. *Letter XXII to Eustochium*, 19; PL 22, 405-406: *Nemo malum bono comparat. Glorientur et nuptæ, cum a virginibus sint secundæ. «Crescite, ait, et multiplicamini, et replete terram» (Genes.1.28). Crescat et multiplicetur ille, qui impleturus est terram. Tuum agmen in cælis est… «Exiet virga de radice Jesse, et flos de radice ejus ascendet» (Isai. 11.1). Virga Mater est Domini, simplex, pura, sincera, nullo extrinsecus germine cohærente, et ad similitudinem Dei unione fecunda. Virgæ flos Christus est, dicens: «Ego flos campi, et lilium convallium» (Cant. 2.1). Qui et in alio loco, lapis prædicatur abscissus de monte sine manibus (Dan. 2), significante Propheta, virginem nasciturum esse de Virgine…*

114 See *Letter 22 to Eustochium*, 21 ; PL 22, 408 : *Postquam vero Virgo*

concepit in utero, et peperit nobis puerum, «cujus principatus in humeros ejus» (Isai. 9.6), Deum, fortem, patrem futuri sæculi, soluta maledictio est. Mors per Evam: vita per Mariam. Ideoque et ditius virginitatis donum fluxit in feminas, quia cœpit a femina. Statim ut filius Dei ingressus est super terram, novam sibi familiam instituit, UT QUI AB ANGELIS adorabatur in cœlo, haberet Angelos et in terris. See also paragraph 18 of the same letter, PL 22, 405: *Mihi virginitas in Maria dedicatur et Christo.*

115 See *On the Perpetual Virginity of Blessed Mary*, 6; PL 23, 191: ... *qui Annam prophetissam, Magos, stellam, Herodem, Angelos viderat; qui, inquam, miracula tanta cognoverat, Dei templum, Spiritus sancti sedem, Domini sui matrem audebat attingere?*

116 See *On the Perpetual Virginity of Blessed Mary, 19*; PL 23, 203.

Sed ut hæc quæ scripta sunt, non negamus, ita ea quæ non sunt scripta, renuimus. Natum Deum esse de Virgine credimus, quia legimus. Mariam nupsisse post partum, non credimus, quia non legimus. Nec hoc ideo dicimus, quo nuptias condemnemus, ipsa quippe virginitas fructus est nuptiarum: sed quod nobis de sanctis viris temere æstimare nihil liceat. Possumus enim hac æstimatione possibilitatis contendere, plures quoque uxores habuisse Joseph, quia plures habuerit Abraham, plures habuerit Jacob; et de his esse uxoribus fratres Domini, quod plerique non tam pia quam audaci temeritate confingunt. Tu dicis Mariam virginem non permansisse: ego mihi plus vindico, etiam ipsum Joseph virginem fuisse per Mariam, ut ex virginali conjugio virgo filius nasceretur. Si enim in virum sanctum fornicatio non ca-

But as we do not deny the things which have been set down in writing, so do we reject the things which have not been recorded. We believe that God was born from a Virgin because we read it. That Mary had marital relations after giving birth we do not believe because we do not read it. And neither do we say this because we reject marital intercourse, for virginity itself is a fruit of marital intercourse: but because we are not permitted to judge thoughtlessly concerning holy men. We can, indeed, in this rash evaluation of what is possible assert that Joseph had multiple wives because Abraham had many wives, as did Jacob; and that the "brothers of the Lord" are from these wives, as many contrive in thoughtlessness resulting not so much from piety as from audacity. You say that Mary did not remain a virgin: I, for my part,

dit, et aliam eum uxorem habuisse non scribitur: Mariæ autem, quam putatus est habuisse, custos potius fuit, quam maritus: relinquitur, virginem eum mansisse cum Maria, qui pater Domini meruit appellari.

claim further that Joseph himself was a virgin for the sake of Mary, so that a virgin son should be born from a virginal marriage. If, indeed, adultery never befell the holy man, and it is not written that he had another wife; and he was the guardian, rather than the husband, of Mary, whom he was thought to have had as wife: it follows that he who merited to be called the father of the Lord remained a virgin along with Mary.

St. Jerome will further develop his high view of St. Joseph's nobility in his *Commentary on the Gospel of St. Matthew* (book 1, chap. 1; PL 26, 24) in which he asserts that St. Joseph wanted to dismiss Mary not because he suspected her of adultery, but, rather, due to a deep reverential fear for the incomprehensible mystery that he saw unfolding in her:

Si quis fornicariæ conjungitur, unum corpus efficitur (1 Cor. VI, 16). Et in Lege præceptum est, non solum reos, sed et conscios criminum obnoxious esse peccati (Levit. V): quomodo Joseph cum crimen celet uxoris, justus scribitur ? Sed hoc testimonium Mariæ est, quod Joseph sciens illius castitatem, et admirans quod evenerat, celat silentio, cujus mysterium nesciebat.

If someone copulates with an adulteress, he becomes one body with her (1 Cor. 6:16). And in the Law, it is a precept that not only those guilty of the sin, but also any who are informed about the sin are punishable for the same crime (Levit. 5). How then is it written that Joseph was just if he concealed his wife's supposed crime? But this serves as proof concerning Mary, that Joseph, being convinced of her chastity, yet filled with wonder at what had transpired, concealed by means of silence a mystery which he did not understand.

117 It is precisely as a satrist that Dante identifies Horace in Canto IV of the *Inferno* (IV, 89). In *De Vulgari Eloquentia* (II, iv), he refers to Horace as "Magister noster Oratius". It seems, moreover, that Dan-

te himself made abundant use of satire in *The Divine Comedy*. One need only think of the masterful way he mocks his Tuscan homeland in Canto XIV of *Purgatorio* by depicting the Arno River as a hideous monster that bends its way around the beastly inhabitants of Arezzo, Florence and Pisa, or Forese's pungent invective against the sleazy clothing of Florentine women in *Purgatorio* XXXIII. If Dante made use of satire, therefore, he was indebted to St. Jerome for having "Christianized" the genre in his writings.

118 John N. Hritzu, Ph.D. See footnote 42 in his General Introduction to *Saint Jerome: Dogmatic and Polemical Works,* Trans. John N. Hritzu, Ph.D., The Catholic University of America Press, Inc., Washington, D.C., 1965. Dr. Hritzu makes reference to an important study made by David S. Wiesen entitled *St. Jerome as a Satirist, a Study of Christian Thought and Letters (Ithaca, New York, 1964).*

119 See the *Commentary on Galatians,* Book 1, Chap. 2; PL 26, 340:

Aliquoties cum adolescentulus Romæ controversias declamarem, et ad vera certamina fictis me litibus exercerem, currebam ad tribunalia judicum, et disertissimos oratorum tanta inter se videbam acerbitate contendere, ut omissis sæpe negotiis, in proprias contumelias verterentur, et joculari se invicem dente morderent.

When as a youth in Rome I would at times rehearse rhetorical delivery by means of arguments, and would train myself for real clashes through simulated lawsuits, I would hasten to the judges' courtrooms, and there would see the most articulate of orators contend among themselves with so much acrimony that they would often put aside their legal matters and resort to mutual invective, and to ridicule each other would, as it were, sink teeth.

120 See *On the Perpetual Virginity of Blessed Mary,* 13, 16; PL 23, 195, 199-200.

O furor cæcus, et in proprium exitium mens vesana! Dicis ad crucem Domini matrem ejus fuisse præsentem, dicis Joanni discipulo ob viduitatem et solitudinem commendatam: quasi juxta te non ha-

O blind fury and senseless mind intent upon its own destruction! You say that at the Lord's cross His Mother was present, you say that she was entrusted to the disciple John on account of her soli-

beret quatuor filios, et innumeras filias, quarum consortio frueretur?

tary widowhood: as if, according to you, she didn't have four sons and countless daughters whose company she could have enjoyed?

Impertissime hominum . . . ad injuriam Virginis tuam rabiem contulisti, in exemplum ejus quem fabulæ ferunt, cum vulgo esset ignotus, et nihil boni posset facinoris excogitare, quo nobilis fieret, Dianæ incendisse templum; et nullo prodente sacrilegium, fertur ipse in medium processisse, clamitans sese incendium subjecisse: sciscitantibus Ephesi principibus, quam ob causam hoc facere voluisset, respondisse: Ut quia bene non poteram, male omnibus innotescerem. Et hoc quidem Græca narrat historia. Tu vero templum Dominici corporis succendisti, tu contaminasti sanctuarium Spiritus Sancti, ex quo vis quadrigam fratrum, et sororum processisse congeriem . . .

Most ignorant of men . . . you took your rabid fury to bring insult to the Virgin, in imitation of him concerning whom the fables speak, that, as he was unknown to the crowds, and could devise no decent deed by which he could win fame, set fire to Diana's temple. And as the sacrilege in no way brought about his purpose, it is reported he came forth into the midst of all and shouted out that he it was who sparked the conflagration. When the governors of Ephesus inquired why he chose to do this, he responded: So that by means of evil I could be well-known, since by means of good I could not do so. And this Greek history actually relates. But you set fire to the temple of the Lord's body, you have contaminated the sanctuary of the Holy Ghost, from which you fancy to have issued forth a four-fold team of brothers and a throng of sisters . . .

Quis, te oro, ante hanc blasphemiam noverat, quis dupondii supputabat? Consecutus es quod volebas, nobilis es factus in scelere. Ego ipse qui contra te scribo, cum in eadem tecum Urbe consistam albus, ut aiunt, aterve sis, nescio. Prætermitto vitia sermonis, qui-

Please, tell me, who even knew you before you uttered forth this blasphemy? Who thought you worth a dime? You've gotten what you wanted, by your heinous deed you've gained renown. I myself, who write against you, though I live with you in the same City, don't

bus omnis liber tuus scatet. Taceo ridiculum exordium. O tempora! O mores!

know if you are white or black, as they say. I pass over the defects of your discourse, with which your whole book teems. I make no mention of your ridiculous first line, *O tempora! O mores!*

121 See *Letter 48 to Pammachius*, 18; PL 22, 508: *Dum adviveret sanctæ memoriæ Damasus, librum contra Helvidium «de Beatæ Mariæ virginitate perpetua» scripsimus, in quo necesse fuit nobis ad virginitatis beatitudinem prædicandam, multa de molestiis dicere nuptiarum. Num vir egregious, et eruditus in Scripturis, et virgo Ecclesiæ virginis doctor, aliquid in illo sermone reprehendit?*

122 Although there is general agreement that St. Jerome wrote this treatise in the year 384, it is less clear as to what time of the year he did so. I have chosen late Spring as a likely moment on the basis of Jerome's *Letter 31 to Eustochium*, in which he thanks her for some small gifts she sent to him on the feast of Sts. Peter and Paul, and in which he makes reference to the previous treatise on Virginity *(pristini libelli)*.

123 See *Letter 127 to Principia*, 5; PL 22, 1090: *Hujus (i.e. Marcellæ) amicitiis fruita est Paula venerabilis. In hujus cubiculo nutrita Eustochium, virginitatis decus: ut facilis æstimatio sit, qualis magistra, ubi tales discipulæ.*

124 As for Prætextata, she at last repented after suffering divine retribution for her sacrilegious attempt to pilfer from Christ one of "His jewels and most precious gems". *See Letter 107 to Læta*, 5; PL 22, 873-874:

Prætextata nobilissima quondam femina, jubente viro Hymetio, qui patruus Eustochii virginis fuit, habitus ejus, cultumque mutavit, et neglectum crinem mundano more texuit, vincere cupiens et virginis propositum, et matris desiderium. Et ecce sibi eadem nocte cernit in somnis venisse Angelum terribili facie minitantem pœnas, et hæc verba frangentem: Tu ne

Prætextata, a woman who was once of great nobility, at the bidding of her husband, Hymetius, Eustochium's paternal uncle, changed the young girl's monastic habit and her pious way of life, and subjected her disheveled head of hair to a worldly make-over, desiring thus to overcome the virgin's purpose and her mother's wish. But lo, that very night she saw in

ausa es viri imperium præferre Christo? Tu caput virginis Dei, tuis sacrilegis attrectare manibus, quæ jam nunc arescent, ut sentias excruciata quid feceris, et finito mense quinto, ad inferna ducaris. Sin autem perseveraveris in scelere, et marito simul orbaberis, et filiis. Omnia per ordinem expleta sunt, et seram miseræ pœnitentiam velox signavit interitus. Sic ulciscitur Christus violatores templi sui: sic gemmas et pretiosissima ornamenta defendit.

dreams an Angel with a terrifying face portending punishment, and who broke forth into these words: *Did you dare prefer to Christ your husband's bidding? You foisted your sacrilegious hands upon the head of she who is God's virgin, and now these hands shall wither, that in suffering you may perceive what you have done, and after five months, you shall be guided down to hell. But if you persist in your transgression, you shall also be deprived of both your husband and your sons.* All these things were realized in strict succession, and a swift decline secured the wretch's overdue repentance. Thus is Christ avenged on those who violate His temple: Thus He guards His jewels and most precious gems.

125 See *Letter 22 to Eustochium*, 1,2; PL 22, 395: *Hoc ergo illud magnum est Sacramentum . . . Hæc idcirco, mi Domina Eustochium, scribo (Dominam quippe vocare debeo sponsam Domini mei) ut ex ipso principio lectionis agnosceres, non me nunc laudem Virginitatis esse dicturum, quam probasti optimam, et consecuta es . . . sed ut intelligeres tibi exeunti de Sodoma, timendum esse Lot uxoris exemplum. Nulla est enim in hoc libello adulatio. Adulator quippe blandus inimicus est.*

126 Jerome relates in *De Viris Illustribus*, 134 (PL 23, 715) Sophronius made the translation. It was to Sophronius, furthermore, that Jerome dedicated his translation of the Psalms from the Hebrew, see the Preface to the work in PL 28, 1125.

127 See *Letter 22 to Eustochium*, 15; PL 22, 403.

128 See *Letter 38 to Marcella*, where the history of Blesilla's conversion is described, PL 22, 463-465.

129 See the *Preface to the Commentary on Ecclesiastes*; PL 23, 1009: *Memini me ante hoc ferme quinquennium, cum adhuc Romæ essem,*

et Ecclesiasten sanctæ Blesillæ legerem, ut eam ad contemptum istius sæculi provocarem, et omne quod in mundo cerneret, putaret esse pro nihilo; rogatum ab ea, ut in morem Commentarioli quæque dissererem, ut absque me posset intelligere, quæ legebat. Itaque quoniam in procinctu nostri operis subita morte subtracta est, et non meruimus, o Paula et Eustochium, talem vitæ nostræ habere consortem, tantoque vulnere tunc perculsus obmutui: nunc in Bethleem positus, augustiori videlicet civitate, et illius memoriæ, et vobis reddo quod debeo.

130 See the consolatory *Letter 39 to Paula,* where the history of Blesilla's admirable life and holy death are recounted (PL 22, 465-473).

131 See *Letter 54 to Furia,* 2; PL 22, 550: *Blæsillamque prætereo, quæ maritum suum, tuum secuta germanum, in brevi vitæ spatio tempora virtutum multa complevit.*

132 See *Letter 108 to Eustochium,* 6; PL 22, 881: *Postquam vir mortuus est, ita eum planxit, ut prope ipsa moreretur…*

133 Cf. *Letter 31 to Eustochium,* 1; PL 22, 445: *Apud Deum enim nihil voluptuosum; nihil tantum suave placet; nisi quod in se habet mordacis aliquid veritatis.*

134 See *Letter 45 to Asella,* 2; PL 22, 481: *Nihil mihi aliud objicitur nisi sexus meus, et hoc nunquam objicitur, nisi quum Jerosolymam Paula proficiscitur. Esto, crediderunt mentienti: cur non credunt neganti? Idem est homo ipse qui fuerat: fatetur insontem, qui dudum noxium loquebatur…* On Jerome's retirement to the country prior to his definitive departure from Rome, see *Letter 43 to Marcella.*

135 In the last letter he wrote before sailing from Italy (Letter 45, 7; PL 22, 483), he asked Asella to greet Paula and Eustochium, who, evidently, were still in Rome.

136 Letter 14 to Heliodorus, PL 22, 347-355.

137 Ibid, 2; PL 22, 348.

Licet parvulus ex collo pendeat nepos, licet sparso crine et scissis vestibus, ubera quibus te nutrierat, mater ostendat, licet in limine pater jaceat, per calcatum perge patrem, siccis oculis ad vexillum crucis evola. SOLUM PIETATIS genus est, in hac re esse crudelem.

Though your infant nephew should dangle from your neck, though your mother should, with tousled hair and garments rent, display the breasts with which she fed you, though your father sprawl himself over the threshold, trampling over him proceed, with tearless eyes make speed unto the

standard of the Cross. OF PIETY there is no other sort, than in this matter to be cruel.

Writing to Marcella concerning Blesilla's conversion (Letter 38, 5; PL 22, 465), Jerome would write: *ET PIETATIS genus est, impium esse pro Domino,* which we could translate: *And a category of Piety is to be impious (i.e. towards one's parents) for the Lord.* See also footnote #7 and St. Jerome's commentary on Matthew 10:37.

138 See *Letter 108 to Eustochium,* 6; PL 22, 881-882.

Non domus, non liberorum, non familiæ, non possessionum, non alicujus rei, quæ ad sæculum pertinet, memor, sola (si dici potest) et incomitata, ad eremum Antoniorum atque Paulorum pergere gestiebat. Tandemque exacta hyeme, aperto mari, redeuntibus ad ecclesias suas episcopis, et ipsa voto cum eis ac desiderio navigavit. Quid ultra differo? Descendit ad portum, fratre, cognatis, affinibus, et quod his majus est, liberis prosequentibus, et clementissimam matrem pietate vincere cupientibus. Jam carbasa tendebantur, et remorum ductu navis in altum protrahebatur. Parvus Toxotius supplices manus tendebat in littore. Ruffina jam nubilis, ut suas exspectaret nuptias, tacens fletibus obsecrabat. Et tamen illa siccos tendebat ad cælum oculos, pietatem in filios, pietate in Deum superans. Nesciebat se matrem, ut Christi probaret ancillam. Torquebantur viscera, et quasi a suis membris distraheretur, cum dolore pugnabat : in eo cunctis admirabilior, quod magnam

Mindful not of home, nor children, nor household, nor possessions, nor any other thing belonging to this world, alone (if this can be said) and unaccompanied, she keenly longed to journey to the desert colonized by many an Anthony and Paul. At last, with winter past, and with the sea accessible and open, as the bishops (i.e. Paulinus and Epiphanius) sailed back to their churches, she also put to sea—although by means of solemn promise and desire. Why should I furthermore delay? She went down to the port with brother, in-laws, relatives, and what is more, with her own children following behind her, desiring to overcome that gentlest of mothers through compassion. The sailing canvas was by now unfurled, and by the rowing of the oars the ship was borne aloft. At the shore the small Toxotius stretched forth beseeching hands. Ruffina, now of marriageable age, and as she hoped to be wed soon, implored with silent sobs. And yet, that

vinceret caritatem. Inter hostium manus et captivitatis duram necessitatem nihil crudelius est, quam parentes a liberis separari. Hoc contra jura naturæ plena fides patiebatur, imo gaudens animus appetebat : et amorem filiorum majore in Deum amore contemnens, in sola Eustochio, quæ et propositi et navigationis ejus comes erat, acquiescebat. Sulcabat interim navis mare, et cunctis qui cum ea vehebantur littora respicientibus, ipsa aversos tenebat oculos, ne videret quos sine tormento videre non poterat. Fateor, nulla sic amavit filios, quibus antequam proficisceretur : cuncta largita est : exhæredans se in terra, ut hæreditatem inveniret in cælo.

woman turned her tearless eyes to heaven, by means of piety towards God defeating piety towards her very children. She was unmindful of her status as a mother to verify she was the handmaid of the Lord. Her bowels turned within her, and with the pain she fought as if she were disjointed from her very members: in this, though, more admirable still was that she conquered love so great. Amidst the hands of enemies and harsh constraints of bondage, nothing is more brutal than for parents to be split up from their children. This, against the laws of nature, a faith robust endured, nay, more, a soul rejoicing sought: and deeming slight love for her children through a greater love for God, she found rest in Eustochium alone, who with her shared one common aim and journey. And as the ship began to plough across the sea, and all those being borne away with her fixed eager gazes at the shore, she firmly turned her eyes away, so that she would not see those whom she could not see without distress. I readily declare, that thus no woman ever loved her children, on whom she lavished all before departing, disinheriting herself on earth, in order to acquire an inheritance in heaven.

139 See *Adversus Rufinum*, III, 22; PL 23, 473: *Vis nosse profectionis meæ de Urbe ordinem ? Narrabo breviter. Mense Augusto, flantibus etesiis, cum sancto Vincentio presbytero, et adolescente fratre, et aliis*

monachis, qui nunc Hierosolymæ commorantur, navim in Romano portu securus ascendi, maxima me Sanctorum frequentia prosequente...

140 See *Letter 24 to Marcella,* on the virtues of the solitary virgin Asella, PL 22, 427-428.

141 See *Letter 45 to Asella;* PL 22, 480-484.

Si tibi putem gratias a me referri posse, non sapiam. Potens est Deus super persona mea sanctæ animæ tuæ restituere quod meretur. Ego enim indignus nec æstimare unquam potui, nec optare, ut mihi tantum in Christo largieris affectum. Et licet me sceleratum quidam putent, et omnibus flagitiis obrutum, et pro peccatis meis, etiam hæc parva sint : tamen tu bene facis, quod ex tua mente etiam malos, bonos putas.

I'd be a fool to think that I could adequately thank you. God is able to repay your holy soul on my behalf that which it merits. Indeed, I am unworthy, and could never have imagined, nor yet hoped, that you would lavish on me such affection in the Lord. And though some may consider me a scoundrel, and submerged beneath a torrent of disgraces—and, though, these even for my sins be slight: in this, however, you do well: that from your heart you reckon noble even the despicable.

142 Ibid. *Ego probrosus, ego versipellis et lubricus: ego mendax et Satanæ arte decipiens.*

143 Ibid.

Hæc, mi domina Asella, cum jam navem conscenderem, raptim flens dolensque conscripsi, et gratias ago Deo meo, quod dignus sum, quem mundus oderit. Ora autem ut de Babylone Jerosolymam regrediar, ne mihi dominetur Nabuchodonosor, sed Jesus filius Josedec: veniat Ezras, qui interpretatur adjutor, et reducat me in patriam meam. Stultus ego qui volebam cantare Canticum Domini in terra aliena, et deserto monte Sina, Ægypti auxilium flagitabam (Jer. 42). Non

With tears and sorrow, now that I have boarded ship, I've quickly written down these things, my Dame, Asella, and I thank my God that I am worthy to be one whom this world hates. Pray, though, that from this Babylon unto Jerusalem I may return, lest Nebuchadnezzar govern me, but, rather, Jesus, the son of Josedec. Let Ezras come, whose name means helper, and lead me once again into my homeland. I am a fool, because I wished to sing the Canticum Domini in

recordabar Evangelii, quia qui de Jerusalem egreditur, statim incidit in latrones, spoliatur, vulneratur, occiditur. Sed licet Sacerdos despiciat atque Levites, Samaritanus ille misericors est (Luc. 10), qui cum diceretur: Samaritanus es et dæmonium habes (Joan. 8), dæmonium renuens, Samaritem se non negavit; quia quem nos custodem, Hebræi samaritem vocant. Maleficum quidam me garriunt: titulum fidei, servus agnosco. Magum vocant, et Judæi Dominum meum. Seductor et Apostolus dictus est. Tentatio me non apprehendat, nisi humana (1. Cor. 10). Quotam partem angustiarum perpessus sum, qui Cruci milito? Infamiam falsi criminis imputarunt: sed scio per bonam et malam famam perveniri ad regna cælorum.

a foreign land, and having left behind Mount Sinai, went beseeching Egypt for assistance (Jer. 42). I forgot the Gospel, that whoever leaves Jerusalem at once falls in with robbers, and is stripped, wounded and slain. And though even the Priest and Deacon look down with disdain, that Samaritan is merciful (Lk. 10), who, when they told him: You're a Samaritan and have a demon (Jn. 8), rejecting the part about the demon, did not object to being a Samaritan, for he whom we call guardian, the Hebrews call Samaritan. Some scandalmongers call me an enchanter; I, a servant of the Lord, accept it as a title of fidelity. The Jews, as well, call my Lord a magician. The Apostle, too, was labeled a seducer. No temptation, save for a human one, has taken hold of me (1 Cor. 10). What trifle of distress have I, who soldier for the Cross, endured? They charged me with the infamy of a false crime: I know, however, that through good and bad repute one can attain unto the realms of heaven.

Saluta Paulam et Eustochium, velit nolit mundus, in Christo meas. Saluta matrem Albinam, sororemque Marcellam, Marcellinam quoque, et sanctam Felicitatem, et dic eis : Ante tribunal Christi simul stabimus, ibi apparebit qua mente quis vixerit. Memento mei,

Greet Paula and Eustochium, who, whether the world wishes it or not, are mine in Christ. Greet your mother Albina, and your sister Marcella, and also Marcellina, and devout Felicity, and tell them: We shall likewise stand before

exemplum pudicitiæ, et virginitatis insigne ; fluctusque maris tuis precibus mitiga.

the judgment seat of Christ, there shall come to light the mindset with which each of us has lived. Remember me, O eminent exemplar of virginity and purity; and by your prayers mitigate the billows of the sea.

CHAPTER 7: JEROME'S SECOND PERIOD IN THE EAST

144 See Adversus Rufinum, III, 22; PL 23, 473: *Vis nosse profectionis meæ de Urbe ordinem ? Narrabo breviter. Mense Augusto, flantibus etesiis, cum sancto Vincentio presbytero, et adolescente fratre, et aliis monachis, qui nunc Hierosolymæ commorantur, navim in Romano portu securus ascendi, maxima me Sanctorum frequentia prosequente. Veni Rhegium, in Scyllæo littore paululum steti, ubi veteres didici fabulas, et præcipitem pellacis Ulyssis cursum, et sirenarum cantica, et insatiabilem Charybdis voraginem. Cumque mihi accolæ illius loci multa narrarent, darentque consilium, ut non ad Protei columnas, sed ad Jonæ portum navigarem : illum enim fugientium et turbatorum, hunc securi hominis esse cursum, malui per Maleas et Cycladas Cyprum pergere. Ubi susceptus a venerabili episcopo Epiphanio, cujus tu testimonio gloriaris, veni Antiochiam, ubi fruitus sum communione pontificis confessorisque Paulini, et deductus ab eo media hyeme et frigore gravissimo, intravi Hierosolymam. Vidi multa miracula ; et quæ prius ad me fama pertulerat, oculorum judicio comprobavi. Inde contendi Ægyptum, lustravi monasteria Nitriæ, et inter Sanctorum choros aspides latere perspexi. Protinus concito gradu Bethleem meam reversus sum, ubi adoravi præsepe et incunabula Salvatoris.*

145 *Letter 108 to Eustochium*, 7 ; PL 22, 882: *Delata ad insulam Pontiam, quam clarissimæ quondam feminarum sub Domitiano Principe pro confessione nominis Christiani, Flaviæ Domitillæ nobilitavit exilium; videnque cellulas in quibus illa longum martyrium duxerat sumptis fidei alis, Jerosolymam et sancta Loca videre cupiebat . . . tandem venit Cyprum, ubi sancti et venerabilis Epiphanii pedibus provoluta, decem ab eo diebus retenta est: non in refectionem, ut ille arbitrabatur, sed in opus Dei, ut re comprobatum est. Nam omni illius regionis lustrans monasteria, prout potuit, refrigeria sumptuum*

fratribus dereliquit, quos amor sancti viri de toto illuc orbe conduxerat.

146 Ibid, 9, 883: *cuncta loca tanto ardore ac studio circumivit, ut nisi ad reliqua festinaret, a primis non posset abduci.*

147 Ibid, 14, 890: *Per singulos sanctos Christum se videre credebat; et quidquid in illos contulerat, in Dominum se contulisse lætabatur. Mirus ardor, et vix in femina credibilis fortitudo. Oblita sexus et fragilitatis corporeæ, inter tot millia Monachorum cum puellis suis habitare cupiebat. Et forsitan cunctis eam suscipientibus, impetrasset, ni majus sanctorum Locorum retraxisset desiderium.*

148 Cf. *Prologue to the Commentary on Hosea*, written twenty two years after the pilgrimage to Alexandria, where he explains to Pammachius, Paula's son-in-law, how he obtained Didymus' commentary on Hosea, PL 25, 819: *Unde ante annos circiter viginti duos, cum rogatu sanctæ et venerabilis socrus, immo matris tuæ Paulæ (illud enim nomen carnis, hoc spiritus est : quæ monasteriorum et Scripturarum semper amore flagravit) essem Alexandriæ, vidi Didymum, et eum frequenter audivi, virum sui temporis eruditissimum, rogavique eum, ut quod Origenes non fecerat, ipse completet, et scriberet in Osee Commentarios : qui tres libros, me petente, dictavit, quinque quoque alios in Zachariam.*

149 Cf. *Prologue to the Commentary on Ephesians*, written shortly after their return from Alexandria, in which he tells Paula and Eustochium that the reason he wanted to go there was to learn from Didymus, PL 26, 439: *Denique nuper ob hanc vel maxime causam Alexandriam perrexi, ut viderem Didymum, et ab eo in Scripturis omnibus quæ habebam dubia sciscitarer.*

150 Cf. *De Viris Illustribus*; PL 23, 705: *Didymus, Alexandrinus, captus a parva ætate oculis, et ob id elementorum quoque ignarus, tantum miraculum sui omnibus præbuit, ut dialecticam quoque, et geometriam, quæ vel maxime visu indigent, usque ad perfectum didicerit. Is plura opera et nobilia conscripsit, commentaries in psalmos omnes, commentarios in Evangelium Matthæi et Joannis, et de Dogmatibus, et contra Arianos libros duos, et de Spiritu sancto librum unum, quem ego in Latinum verti: in Isaiam tomos decem et octo, in Osee, ad me scribens, commentarium libros tres, et in Zachariam, meo rogatu, libros quinque, et commentarios in Job, et infinita alia quæ digerere proprii indicis est.*

151 Cf. *Letter 84 to Pammachius and Oceanus*; PL 22, 745: *Perrexi*

tamen Alexandriam, audivi Didymum, in multis ei gratias ago. Quod nescivi, didici: quod sciebam, illo docente, non perdidi.

152 Cf. *Letter 112 to Augustine*; PL 22, 918: *Prætermitto Didymum videntem meum...* See also the Table of Contents for his *De Viris Illustribus*, PL 23, 607, where he refers to the blind teacher as *Didymus ὁ Βλέπων*.

153 Cf. *Letter 68 to Castrutium*; PL 22, 652: *Beatus Antonius cum a sancto Athanasio, Alexandriæ Episcopo, propter confutationem hæreticorum, in urbem Alexandriam esset accitus, et isset ad eum Didymus vir eruditissimus, captus oculis, inter cæteras sermocinationes, quas de Scripturis sanctis habebant, cum ejus admiraretur ingenium, et acumen animi collaudaret, sciscitans ait: Num tristis es, quod oculis carnis careas? Cum ille pudore reticeret; secondo tertioque interrogans, tandem elicuit, ut mœrorem animi simpliciter fateretur. Cui Antonius: Miror, ait, prudentem virum ejus rei dolere damno, quam formicæ et muscæ et culices habent, et non lætari illius possessione, quam sancti soli et Apostoli meruerunt.*

154 See *Letter 108 to Eustochium*, 10; PL 22, 884-885.

Deinde pro facultatula sua, pauperibus atque conservis pecunia distributa, perrexit Bethleem... et in specum Salvatoris introiens, postquam vidit sacrum virginis diversorium, et stabulum in quo *agnovit bos possessorem suum, et asinus præsepe Domini sui (Isai. 1.3)*. . . me audiente jurabat, cernere se oculis fidei infantem pannis involutum, vagientem in præsepi Dominum, Magos adorantes, stellam fulgentem desuper, matrem Virginem *(Matt.2)*, nutricium sedulum, pastores nocte venientes, ut viderent verbum quod factum erat *(Luc. 2.16)*; et jam tunc Evangelistæ Joannis principium dedicarent: *In principio erat Verbum*, et *Verbum caro factum est (Joan. 1)*; parvu-

Then according to her scanty means, as she gave her money to the poor, her fellow servants, she made her way to Bethlehem... and walking in the Savior's cave, after she beheld the Virgin's hostel, and the stable in which *the ox knew his owner and the ass his master's crib (Is. 1:3)* . . . I heard her solemnly declare that with the eyes of faith she saw the infant wrapped in swaddling clothes, the Lord crying in the manger, the Magi adoring Him, the star shining above, the Virgin Mother, their guardian (i.e. St. Joseph) solicitous for them, the shepherds coming in the night to see the Word which had been made (Luc. 2:16); and thus, affirm already the beginning of John's

los interfectos, Herodem sævientem, Joseph et Mariam fugientes in Ægyptum: mixtisque gaudio lacrymis, loquebatur: Salve *Bethleem, domus panis,* in qua natus est ille panis, qui de cælo descendit. Salve *Ephrata*, regio *uberrima*, atque καρποφόρε, cujus fertilitas Deus est. De te quondam Michæas vaticinatus est: *Et tu Bethleem domus Ephrata, non mimina es in millibus Juda. Ex te mihi egredietur, qui sit princeps in Israel : et egressus ejus ab initio a diebus æternitatis (Mich. 5.2.3).* In te enim natus princeps, qui ante Luciferum genitus est *(Psal. 109)* : cujus de Patre nativitas, omnem excedit ætatem . . . Et ego misera atque peccatrix, digna sum judicata deosculari præsepe, in quo Dominus parvulus vagiit? orare in spelunca, in qua virgo puerpera Dominum fudit infantem? Hæc requies mea, quia Domini mei patria est. Hic habitabo, quoniam Salvator elegit eam ... juxta quam Jacob pavit greges suos, et pastores, nocte vigilantes audire meruerunt: *Gloria in excelsis Deo, et super terram pax hominibus bonæ voluntatis (Luc. 2.14).* Dumque servant oves, invenerunt Agnum Dei puro et mundissimo vellere, quod in ariditate totius terræ cœlesti rore complutum est (Judic. 6.37).

Gospel: *In the beginning was the Word, and the Word was made flesh (Jn. 1);* then the slaughtered children, Herod plotting cruelty, Joseph and Mary fleeing into Egypt: and mingling joy with tears, would say: Hail *Bethlehem, house of bread,* in which was born that Bread who from the heavens condescended. Hail *Ephrata*, plentiful and lavish kingdom, rich in choicest fruits, whose fruitfulness is God Himself. Once concerning you Micah foretold: *And Thou, BETHLEHEM Ephrata, art a little one among the thousands of Juda; out of thee shall he come forth unto me that is to be the ruler in Israel: and his going forth is from the beginning, from the days of eternity. (Mic. 5:2-3).* In you, indeed, was born the Prince, who prior to the day star was begotten (Ps. 109): He, whose birth is from the Father and transcends all ages... And is it possible that I, a wretched sinner, have been found worthy to kiss that manger wherein the Newborn Lord first cried? To pray, moreover, in the cave in which the childbearing Virgin brought forth the Infant Lord? Here shall be my resting place, for it is my Lord's fatherland. Here shall I dwell, for it the Savior chose . . . Close to it Jacob fed his flocks, and shepherds keeping watch at night deserved to hear: *Gloria in excelsis Deo et in terra pax hominibus bonæ voluntatis (Lk. 2:14).* And as they kept their

sheep, they came upon the Lamb of God in pure and spotless fleece, which rained upon the arid earth in a celestial dewfall (Jd. 6:37).

155 *Letter 46 of Paula and Eustochium to Marcella*, 10; PL 22, 490.

Verum ut ad villulam Christi, et Mariæ diversorium veniamus quo sermone, qua voce speluncam tibi possumus Salvatoris exponere? Et illud præsepe, in quo infantulus vagiit, silentio magis, quam infirmo sermone honorandum est . . . Ecce in hoc parvo terræ foramine, cœlorum conditor natus est: hic involutus pannis, hic visus a pastoribus, hic demonstratus a stella, hic adoratus a Magis.

And truly when it comes to Christ's small village, and Mary's hostel, what word, what utterance could adequately set forth the Savior's cave? And that manger crib, in which the blessed Infant first gave forth his sobs, is honored more by silence than unsteady words . . . Behold in this small burrow of the earth, the Maker of heaven was born; here He was wrapped in swaddling clothes, here He was seen by shepherds, here He was shown by a star, here He was adored by the Magi.

156 Cf. *Letter 54 to Furia*; PL 22, 557: *Habeat Roma, quod augustior urbe Romana possidet Bethleem; Commentary on Ecclesiastes*, Prologue; PL 23, 1010: *nunc in Bethlehem positus, augustiori videlicet civitate;* Preface to Translation of Didymus' *De Spiritu Sancto;* PL 23, 103: *augustiorem multo locum existimans, qui Salvatorem mundi, quam qui fratris genuit parricidiam;* Letter 58 to Paulinus of Nola; PL 22, 581: *Bethleem nunc nostram, et augustissimum orbis locum...*

157 *Letter 88 to Paulinus of Nola*; PL 22, 580-581.

Non Jerosolymis fuisse, sed Jerosolymis bene vixisse, laudandum est. Illa expetenda, illa laudanda est civitas, non quæ occidit Prophetas, et Christi sanguinem fudit ; sed quam fluminis impetus lætificat (Ps. 45.4 ; Luc. 11) : quæ in monte sita, cælari non potest : quam matrem sanctorum Apostolus clamitat : in qua se municipa-

It is not praiseworthy simply to have been in Jerusalem, but to have lived well in Jerusalem. That city is to be sought, that city is to be praised which is made joyful by the flowing of the river (Ps. 45:4; Lk. 11): which is placed on top of the mountain so that it cannot be concealed: which the Apostle calls the mother of the saints, and in which

tum cum justis lætatur habere.

Neque vero hoc dicens, memtipsum inconstantiæ redarguo, damnoque quod facio : ut frustra videar ad exemplum Abraham, et meos et patriam relinquisse : sed non audeo Dei omnipotentiam angusto fine concludere, et coarctare parvo terræ loco, quem non capit cœlum. Singuli quique credentium, non locorum diversitatibus, sed fidei merito ponderantur. Et veri adoratores, neque Jerosolymis, neque in monte Garizim adorant Patrem : quia Deus Spiritus est, et adoratores ejus in spiritu et veritate adorare oportet. « Spirtus autem spirat ubi vult. Domini est terra et plenitudo ejus » (Joan. 3.8 ; Ps. 23.1) . . . Et Crucis igitur et Resurrectionis loca prosunt his, qui portant crucem suam ; et cum Christo resurgunt quotidie ; qui dignos se tanto exhibent habitaculo. Cæterum qui dicunt : *Templum Domini, Templum Domini (Jer. 7)*, audiant ab Apostolo : *Vos estis templum Domini, et Spiritus Sanctus habitat in vobis (2 Cor. 6.16)*. Et de Jerosolymis et de Britania æqualiter patet aula cœlestis : *Regnum enim Dei intra vos est.*

he rejoices to have citizenship with the souls of the just.

But in saying this I do not rebuke myself of inconstancy, nor condemn that which I do: as if it had been futile that I abandoned family and homeland in imitation of Abraham: but rather, I dare not enclose the omnipotence of God in narrow boundaries, nor restrict Him whom the heavens cannot contain in a tiny corner of the earth. Every believer will be assessed by the merit of his faith, not by the diversity of his dwelling. What is more, the true worshippers adore the Father neither in Jerusalem nor on Mt. Garizim: for God is spirit, and His worshippers must worship in spirit and in truth. "But the Spirit breathes where He wills. The Lord's is the earth and the fullness thereof" (Jn. 3:8; Ps. 23:1) . . . Consequently, the places of both the Cross and the Resurrection avail those who daily bear their cross, and daily rise with Christ, those who show themselves to be His worthy dwelling places. For the rest, let those who say, *it is the Temple of the Lord, the Temple of the Lord* (Jer. 7), hear the Apostle say: *You are the Lord's temple, and the Holy Spirit dwells within you (2 Cor. 6:16)*. And the gates of heaven are equally open to both Jerusalem and Brittany, for *The Kingdom of God is within you.*

158 *Letter 48 to Desiderium*; PL 22, 492: *Lecto sermone Dignitatis tuæ, quem mihi nec opinanti tua benevolentia tribuit, gavisus quidem sum testimonio honesti et eloquentis viri: sed in memet reversus, satis dolui, indignum tantis laudibus atque præconio opprimi me potius quam levari. Scis enim dogma nostrum, humilitatis tenere vexillum, et per ima gradientes, ad summa nos scandere.*

159 See the following:
Letter 57 to Pammachius; PL 22, 579: *Porro mihi sufficit amicum instruxisse carissimum: et in cellula latitantem diem tantum exspectare judicii.*
Letter 75 to Theodora; PL 22, 688: *Nos...qui parvuli et minimi Christianorum sumus, et ob conscientiam peccatorum, Bethleemitici ruris saxa incolimus ...*
Treatise Against John of Jerusalem, PL 23, 394: *Ecclesiam scindere dicimur, qui extra cellulas nostras locum Ecclesiæ non habemus?*
Letter 82 to Theophilus; PL 22, 739: *Nomen meum absque ullis officiis, quibus non invicem palpare solemus homines, frequenter assumitur, carpitur, ventilatur, quasi de libro viventium deletus sim: quasi illius me litteræ suggillaverint; aut istiusmodi nugas umquam quæsierim, qui ab adolescentia in Monasterii clausus cellulis, magis esse voluerim aliquid, quam videri.*
Letter 117 to a Mother and Daughter in Gaul; PL 22, 953: *Quasi vero Episcopalem cathedram teneam, et non clausus cellula, ac procul a turbis remotus, vel præterita plangam vitia, vel vitare nitar præsentia. Sed et incongruum est latere corpore, et lingua per totum orbem vagari.*

160 *Against John of Jerusalem*; PL 23, 395: *Nos scindimus Ecclesiam, qui ante paucos menses...quadraginta diversæ ætatis et sexus, presbyteris tuis obtulimus baptizandos?*

161 *Against Rufinus*, Book III, 17; PL 23, 469: *Nobis in monasterio hospitalitas cordi est; omnesque ad nos venientes, læta humanitatis fronte suscipimus. Veremur enim ne Maria cum Joseph locum non inveniat in diversorio, ne nobis Jesus dicat exclusus: Hospes eram, et non suscepistis me (Matth. XXV, 43). Solos hæreticos non recipimus, quos vos solos recipitis.*

162 Dialogue I, PL 20, 189: *Oderunt eum hæretici, quia eos impugnare non desinit...*

163 Preface to his translation of Job from the LXX; PL 29, 61-62: *Si*

aut fiscellam junco texerem, aut palmarum folia complicarem, ut in sudore vultus mei comederem panem, et ventris opus sollicita mente tractarem: nullus morderet, nemo reprehenderet. Nunc autem quia juxta sententiam Salvatoris volo operari cibum, qui non periit, et antiquam divinorum Voluminum viam, sentibus virgultisque purgare, mihi genuinus infigitur: corrector visitorum falsarius vocor, et errores non auferre, sed serere. Tanta est enim vetustatis consuetudo, ut etiam confessa plerisque vitia placeant, dum magis pulchros habere malunt codices, quam emendatos. Quapropter, o Paula et Eustochium, unicum nobilitatis et humilitatis exemplar, pro flabello, calathis, sportellisque munusculo monachorum, spiritualia hæc et mansura dona suscipite: ac beatum Job qui adhuc apud Latinos jacebat in stercore, et vermibus scatebat errorum, integrum, immaculatumque gaudete... Nec non et illa quæ habere videbamur, et ita corrupta errant, ut sensum legentibus tollerent, orantibus vobis, magno labore correxi; magis utile quid ex otio meo Christi Ecclesiis venturum ratus, quam ex aliorum negotio.

164 Dialogue I, PL 20, 190: *Totus semper in lectione, totus in libris est: non die, non nocte requiescat; aut legit aliquid semper, aut scribit.*

165 Ibid, 189: *Ecclesiam loci illius Hieronymus presbyter regit: nam parochia est episcopi, qui Hierosolymam tenet*

166 Cf. Preface to his translation of Paralipomenon, PL 28, 1326: *Cæterum memini, editionem Septuaginta Translatorum olim de Græco emendatam tribuisse me nostris: nec inimicum debere æstimari eorum, quos in conventu fratrum semper edissero.* Also Letter 112 to Augustine, *Tres simul epistolas*, PL 22, 931: *Tu qui juvenis es, et in Pontificali culmine constitutes, doceto populos, et novis Africæ frugibus Romana tecta locupletato. Mihi sufficit cum auditore et lectore pauperculo in angulo monasterii susurrare.*

167 Dialogue I, PL 20, 188: *Illud me admodum permovebat, quod Hieronymus, vir maxime catholicus et sacræ legis peritissimus, Origenem secutus primo tempore putabatur, quem nunc idem præcipue, vel omnia illius scripta damnaret.*

168 Letter 33 to Paula, *Marcum Terrentium Varronem*, in praise of Origen and a list of some of his works (PL 22, 446-448), and Letter 43 to Marcella, *Ambrosius, quo chartas*, on his retreat to the countryside and in praise of Origen (PL 22, 478-480).

169 In addition to the Commentary on Ephesians itself (PL 26, 439-554), see the first book of his apology against Rufinus (PL

23, 441-420), in which he outlines for us how his commentary on Ephesians should be read.

170 See his *Panarion*, Hæres. 63 and 64 (PG 41, 1061-1290).

171 For a fascinating accout of Epiphanius's influence over the monks of Egypt and Palestine, see Georges Florovsky's articles *The Anthropomorphites in the Egyptian Desert* and especially the second part of the article, *Theophilus of Alexandria and Apa Aphou of Pemdje* in *Aspects of Church History, Volume Four*, pp. 89-129.

172 See the Apology against John of Jerusalem, 27-35 passim (PL 23, 379-388).

173 *Commentary on Matthew*, Lib. III, Cap. 18; PL 26, 129.

Igitur omnis truncatur affectus, et universa propinquitas amputatur, ne per occasionem pietatis unusquisque credentium scandalis pateat. Si, inquit, ita est quis tibi conjunctus ut manus, pes, oculus, et est utilis atque sollicitus, et acutus ad perspiciendum : scandalum autem tibi facit, et propter dissonantiam morum te pertrahit in gehennam : melius est, ut et propinquitate ejus, emolumentis carnalibus careas, ne, dum vis lucrifacere cognatos et necessarios, causam habeas ruinarum.

Therefore, let every affection be cut off, and every close relation amputated, lest on the grounds of religion any of the faithful suffer scandal. If, he says, someone is so closely connected to you as hand, foot or eye, and is beneficial and attentive, and keenly perceptive, but, nevertheless, causes you scandal, and through inharmonious lifestyle leads you into hell: it is better, nevertheless, that you be deprived of his closeness and the advantages of the flesh that he procures for you, lest, as you seek to save your relatives and friends, you have cause for ruin.

This passage is preserved for us as a homily for the third nocturn of Matins for the feast of St. Michael in the Monastic Breviary. St. Epiphanius would write similar words to John of Jerusalem (Letter 51, PL 22, 520): *Simpliciter loquor: nos secundum quod scriptum est, nec oculo nostro parcimus, ut non effodiamus eum, si nos scandalizaverit: nec manui, neque pedi, si nobis scandalum fecerit. Et vos ergo sive oculi nostril, sive manus, sive pedes fueritis, similia sustinebitis.* See also the following passage from Jerome's commentary on the Gospel of Matthew (PL 26, col. 68):

Qui amat patrem aut matrem plus quam me, non est me dignus. Et qui

He who loves father or mother more than me is not worthy of me. And

amat filium aut filiam super me, non est me dignus. Qui ante præmiserat : *Non veni pacem mittere super terram, sed gladium;* et dividere homines adversum patrem et matrem, et socrum, ne quis pietatem religioni anteferret, subjecit dicens : *Qui amat patrem aut matrem plus quam me.* Et in Cantico legimus Canticorum : *Ordinate in me charitatem (Cant. II,4).* Hic ordo in omni affectu necessarius est. Ama post Deum patrem, ama matrem, ama filios. Si autem necessitas venerit, ut amor parentum ac filiorum Dei amori comparetur, et non possit utrumque servari, odium in suos, pietas in Deum sit. Non ergo prohibuit amare patrem aut matrem, sed signanter addidit: *Qui amat patrem aut matrem plus quam me.*

whosoever loves son or daughter more than me, is not worthy of me. He who before had laid down: *I did not come to bring peace upon earth, but, rather, a sword;* and divide men from father and mother, and mother-in-law, lest someone should value the piety shown towards relatives more than the piety owed to God, he added: *He who loves father or mother more than me.* And in the Canticle of Canticles we read: *Order charity within me (Cant. 2:4).* This order is necessary in all love. Love your father and mother and children after God. If the force of circumstance should set the love of parents or children side by side with the love of God such that they mutually exclude each other, let hate be shown to your kin, but piety preserved unto God. He did not, therefore, forbid loving father or mother, but qualified this love by adding: *He who loves father or mother more than me.*

174 See *Against Rufinus,* book III, ch. 33 (PL 23, 481-482).

175 See Letter 51 from Epiphanius to John of Jerusalem, *Oportebat nos,* 1 (PL 22, 518): *invenire autem, et comprehendere servum Dei non posses, qui te, eo quod grave onus sacerdotii nollet suscipere, sæpe fugiebat: sed nec alius quis Episcoporum facile eum reperiret.*

176 Ibid: *Unde, et satis miratus sum, quomodo dispensatione Dei ad nos venerit cum Diaconis monasterii, et cæteris fratribus, ut mihi satisfaceret, quia nescio quid adversum eos habebam tristitiæ.*

177 *Letter 51 from Epiphanius to John of Jerusalem,* 1; PL 22, 518.

. . . ignorantem eum, et nullam penitus habentem suspicionem, per multos Diaconos apprehendi

I gave order by means of many Deacons to seize him—he being entirely oblivious and entertaining

jussimus, et teneri os ejus, ne forte liberari se cupiens, adjuraret nos per nomen Christi: et primum Diaconum ordinavimus, proponents ei timorem Dei, et compellentes, ut ministraret; valde quippe obnitebatur, indignum se esse clamitans, et grave onus ultra vires suas esse contestans. Vix ergo compulimus eum, et persuadere potuimus testimoniis Scripturarum, et propositione mandatorum Dei. Et cum ministrasset in sanctis sacrificiis, rursus cum ingenti difficultate tento ore ejus, ordinavimus Presbyterum: et iisdem verbis, quibus antea suaseramus, impulimus ut sederet in ordine Presbyterii.

no suspicion whatsoever that this would happen— and commanded them to cover his mouth, lest perchance, desiring to escape, he should adjure us in the name of Christ. And first we ordained him a Deacon, setting before him the fear of God and compelling him to exercise the sacred ministry. He greatly persisted in crying out that he was unworthy, and saying that it was a heavy burden which exceeded his strength. We only barely, therefore, coerced him, and were able to persuade him with the witness of the Scriptures, and brought before him the comandments of God. And when he had ministered in the holy sacrifices, we then, again with great difficulty and holding his mouth, ordained him Priest: and we used the same words as before to persuade him, and urged him to sit among those of Priestly rank.

[178] *Letter 51.*

Post hæc scripsimus ad sanctos Presbyteros monasterii, et cæteros fratres : et increpavimus eos, quare non scripsissent super eo, cum ante annum multos eorum queri audissem, cur non haberent, qui sibi Domini sacramenta conficerent, et illum omnes suo poscerent testimonio, et grandem utilitatem in commune monasterii testarentur : quare tunc reperta opportunitate non scripsissent nobis, neque super ordinatione ejus aliquid poposcissent.

Then we wrote to the Priests of the monastery, and other brothers: and rebuked them as to why they had not written to us about him, since before that year I heard many of the brothers complain that they had nobody to consecrate the Eucharist for them, and they all with one accord asked him (i.e. Paulinian) to do it, and attested to the great benefit he would bring to the common good of the monastery.

179 *Letter 51.*

Cum enim vidissem, quia multitudo sanctorum fratrum in monasterio consisteret, et sancti Presbyteri Hieronymus, et Vincentius propter verecundiam, et humilitatem nollet debita nomini suo exercere sacrificia, et laborare in hac parte ministerii, quæ Christianorum præcipua salus est…

While, indeed, I saw that a multitude of holy brothers dwelt in the monastery, and that the holy Priests Jerome and Vincent, on account of their reverent modesty and humility, wished not to perform the sacrifices that fall to their title, and to labor in this part of the sacred ministry which constitutes the chief salvation of Christians…

180 See *Against John of Jerusalem*, 42 (PL 23, 394): *An non tu scindis Ecclesiam, qui mandas clericis tuis, ut si quis Paulinianum ab Epiphanio episcopo consecratum presbyterum dixerit, Ecclesiam prohibeatur intrare. Ex quo tempore usque in præsentem diem videmus tantum specum Domini; et hæreticis intrantibus, procul positi suspiramus.*

181 The most important of these letters (# 51 from Epiphanius to John of Jerusalem, *Oportebat nos*, PL 22, 517-527) was translated by Jerome into Latin for the brothers of his monastery who could not read Greek, and is extant in only this translation. This translation, however, was made exclusively for Jerome's community, and was never intended to be released to the public. However, it subsequently found its way into the hands of John and Rufinus, who alleged Jerome had mistranslated Epiphanius' words. Jerome was understandably upset, first that someone (perhaps Rufinus himself) had stolen the letter from Jerome's monastery, but more importantly, that they accused him of mistranslating Epiphanius. Once word got to Rome about this mess, Pammachius, Jerome's spiritual son and Paula's son-in-law, asked him to explain what happened. He did so in a monumental letter in which he explains in detail the art of translation, Letter 57 to Pammachius, *Paulus Apostolus*, PL 22, 568-579.

182 Cf. *The Sayings of the Desert Fathers*, Trans. Benedicta Ward, SLG Cistercian Publications, 1975. See the following sayings: from Saint Arsenius 7-8 (p. 10); 28 (p. 13); from Saint Epiphanius 2 (p. 57); from Archbishop Theophilus himself pp. 80-82; and finally, from Isidore the Priest 8 (p. 97). This Isidore, whose meeting with

Theophilus is recalled, is most likely the Isidore Theophilus sent to investigate the situation between John and Jerome, but as he was in favor of Origen sided decidedly in favor of John, much to Jerome's chagrin. When Theophilus became an enemy of the Origenists he would eventually banish Isidore from the desert along with the other Origenists living there.

183 *Letter 82 to Theophilus*; PL 22, 736-743.

184 *Letter 82*; PL 22, 737.

Nos nec Ecclesiam scindimus, neque a patrum communione dividimur: sed ab ipsis, ut ita dicam, incunabilis catholico sumus lacte nutriti. Nemo namque magis Ecclesiasticus est, quam qui nunquam hæreticus fuit. Sed ignoramus absque caritate pacem, sine pace communionem. Legimus quoque in Evangelio: *Si offers munus tuum ad altare, et ibi recordatus fueris, quia frater tuus habet aliquid adversum te, dimitte ibi munus tuum coram altari, et vade prius reconciliari fratri tuo; et tunc veniens, offer munus tuum (Matth. 5.13.24)*. Si munera nostra absque pace offerre non possumus: quanto magis et Christi corpus accipere? Qua conscientia ad Eucharistiam Christi accedam, et respondebo Amen, dum de caritate dubitem porrigentis?

We neither split the Church, nor divide ourselves from communion with our forefathers: but from the very cribs of our infancy, if I may say so, we have been nourished on Catholic milk. No one is a greater man of the Church than he who was never a heretic. But we do not recognize peace without charity, nor communion without peace. We also read in the Gospel: *If you bring your gift to the altar, and there remember that your brother has something against you, leave your gift there before the altar, and go first to be reconciled with your brother; then come and offer your gift (Mt. 5:13,24)*. If we cannot make our offering without peace, how much the less can we accept the Body of Christ without it? In what state of conscience can I draw near to the Eucharist, and respond Amen, if I doubt the charity of the one who administers it to me?

185 For a full account of this series of events, see Georges Florovsky's articles *The Anthropomorphites in the Egyptian Desert* and especially the second part of the article, *Theophilus of Alexandria and Apa Aphou of Pemdje* in *Aspects of Church History, Volume Four*, pp. 89-129.

186 *Against John of Jerusalem*, 41; PL 23, 395.

Si causa discordiæ, non ex dissensione fidei est, sed ex Pauliniani, ut dicis, ordinatione descendit, quæ tanta stultitia est volentibus occasionem dare, nolle respondere? Confitere fidem; sed tamen responde quod quæreris, ut omnibus luceat, non de fide, sed de ordinatione esse certamen. Quamdiu enim interrogatus de fide, tacueris, potest tibi adversarius dicere : Non ordinationis causa est, sed fidei. Si ordinationis causa est, stulte facis interrogatus de fide, tacere. Si fidei, stulte prætendis ordinationem. Porro quod dicis te petisse, ut subjicerentur Ecclesiæ Dei, et non scinderent eam, neque proprium sibi facerent principatum, de quibus dicas, non satis intelligo. Si de me et de Presbytero Vincentio, satis multo dormisti tempore, qui post annos tredecim, nunc excitatus hæc loqueris. Ob id enim et ego Antiochiam, et ille Constantinopolim, urbes celeberrimas deseruimus, non ut te in populis prædicantem laudaremus : sed ut in agris et in solitudine adolescentiæ peccata deflentes, Christi in nos misericordiam deflecteremus. Sin autem de Pauliniano tibi sermo est : vides eum Episcopo suo esse subjectum, versari Cypri, ad visitationem nostram interdum venire : non ut tuum, sed ut alienum ; ejus videlicet, a quo ordinatus est. Quod si hic etiam esse

If the discord arose not from a discrepancy of faith, but, as you assert, from Paulinian's ordination, what great foolishness is that which refuses to give an answer to those who want one, thereby strengthening their cause? Confess the faith; but respond, nonetheless, to that which is asked of you, so that it may be evident to all that this conflict is not about faith, but about the ordination. As long as you are interrogated about the faith and you keep silent, your opponent can say to you: This is not about the ordination, but about faith. If the cause of the discord is the ordination, you are foolish to keep silent when questioned about faith. If the discord is about faith, then it is foolish to pretend that it is about the ordination. When you say, moreover, that you asked that "they" be subject to the Church of God, and neither tear it apart, nor make a kingdom for themselves, I have no idea concerning whom you say this. If you meant myself and the Priest Vincent, you have been asleep for quite a long time, for you say this now, 13 years after we settled in Bethlehem. Indeed, the reason I forsook Antioch and he Constantinople, both renowned cities, was not to praise your eloquent preaching among the people, but so that, weeping over the sins of our youth amidst the fields and the

voluerit, et in exsilio nostro quietus in solitudine vivere, quid tibi debet, nisi honorem quem omnibus debemus episcopis ? Fac a te ordinatum : idem ab eo audies, quod a me misello homine sanctæ memoriæ episcopus Paulinus audivit. « Num rogavi te, ut ordinarer ? Si sic presbyterium tribuis, ut monachum nobis non auferas, tu videris de judicio tuo. Sin autem sub nomine presbyteri tollis mihi, propter quod sæculum dereliqui : ego habeo quod semper habui : nullum dispendium in ordinatione passus es. »

solitude of the desert, we might call down upon us the mercy of Christ. If, however, you were referring to Paulinian, know that he is subject to his bishop and living in Cyprus, and comes every now and then to visit us, not as one of your priests, but as that of another, i.e. of him who ordained him. But even if he desired to be here, and peacefully dwell in solitude partaking of our exile, what does he owe you if not the honor which we owe all bishops? Say that you ordained him: you would hear the same thing from him as that which the bishop Paulinus of blessed memory heard from me, a wretch of a man: "Did I ask you to be ordained? If in conferring the priesthood you do not deprive us of the monastic state, do as it seems best to you. But if by the title of priest you divest me of that on account of which I forsook the world, I keep that which I have always had: you sustained no losses in this ordination."

187 *Commentary on Ezechiel*, Book XI, Chapter XXXIV; PL 25, 330. The last psalm verse quoted by Jerome is incorrectly noted by the Migne edition as coming from Psalm 102; it comes, in fact, from Psalm 146:3 (Ps. CXLVI, 3).

Tunc educentur de terris, ut inducantur in terram suam, quæ est terra viventium : et ipse eas pascet in montibus Israel, de quibus loquitur David: Levavi oculos meos in montes, unde veniet auxilium mihi (Ps. CXX, 1). Et non so-

Then shall they be led into their land—the land of those who truly live—from all the nations: and He will feed them on the peaks of Israel, concerning which David declares: "I lifted up my eyes unto the mountains, whence my help

lum in montibus, ed in rivis, et in cunctis sedibus terræ, in pascuis uberrimis, et in monte excelso, de quo Isaias, et Michæas plenius vaticinantur (Isa. II ; Mich. IV, VII) : sive in montibus excelsis Israel. Ibi requiescent in herbis virentibus, et dicent: Dominus pascit me, et nihil mihi deerit : in loco pascuæ ibi me collocavit : Super aquas refectionis educavit me (Ps. XXII, 1,2). Et pascentur in pascuis pinguissimis super montes Israel. Est infinita promissio, spesque beatitudinis, quando ipse Dominus pollicetur dicens : Ego pascam oves meas ; et nequaquam eas committam malis pastoribus, et ego eas accubare faciam, dicit Dominus Deus, ut requiescant in sinu Abraham, Isaac et Jacob. Tunc quod perierat in gentium populis, requiretur : et quod erraverat in hæreticorum persuasione, reducetur : et quod fractum fuerat, alligabitur : et quod contritum, atque infirmum, consolidabitur ; ut impleatur quod scriptum est : Qui sanat infirmitates eorum, et alligat contritiones eorum (Ps. CII, 3).

comes" (Ps. 120:1) . . . There shall they rest on verdant meadows and shall say: "The Lord feeds me, and nothing shall be wanting unto me: in wholesome pastures He shall settle me: He led me forth upon the waters of refreshment" (Ps. 22:1,2). And there they shall be fed upon the most abundant pastures of Israel's mountains. We are given an infinite promise, and hope of beatitude, when the Lord assures us, saying: I shall feed my sheep; and shall entrust them by no means to wicked shepherds, and I shall make them lie down, says the Lord God, that they may rest in the bosom of Abraham, Isaac and Jacob. Then that which had been lost among the Gentiles shall be sought: and that which went astray in the persuasion of the heretics shall be brought back: the injured and the ailing shall be strengthened; that what is written may be brought to pass: "Who heals all their infirmities, and bandages their injuries."

EPILOGUE

188 *The Saint Francis of Assisi Omnibus of Sources*, Ed. Marion A. Habig, Franciscan Herald Press, Chcago, Illinois, 1983; pp. 710-711.